A KARATE STORY

Thirty Years in the Making

Seamus O'Dowd

Published by Nintai Publications

Printed by CreateSpace

CONTENTS

CONTENTS

ACKNOWLEDGEMENTS

I would like to acknowledge the assistance of the following people who have helped me along the way, in and out of the dojo.

My mother (Myra), father (Mattie) and brothers (Brendan, Des and Enda).

My wife, Nicola – my soulmate.

My children, Conall, Cliona, Aisling and Alva – my inspiration.

My first Sensei, Ray Payne, and all at Bandon Karate Club, past and present.

Kanazawa Soke, all of the SKIF Honbu Dojo instructors, and my many friends in SKIF all over the world.

Sensei Stan Schmidt, Sensei Dave Friend, and all my friends in the JKA in South Africa and Australia.

Garry Cashman – my karate brother.

All my students at Shin-Do-Kan, past and present.

The members and committee of SKIF Ireland, and especially Kevin Sullivan for all of his help.

Ruth Callinan and Djinn von Noorden – for their assistance in editing this book.

DEDICATION

I started writing this book while taking my turn watching over my father when he was ill. I tried writing some articles for my blog, but my mind kept wandering back to my younger days, so I ended up writing about the past. Before I knew it, I had written a big chunk of this book, and I decided to just keep going.

I am well aware that there are many people in karate who are far senior to me, and who have had far more interesting experiences than I have. This book was written as a personal account, and if people enjoy reading it then all the better.

I dedicate this book firstly to my father, Mattie O'Dowd (RIP) – my first hero.

I dedicate it secondly to my sensei, Kanazawa Hirokazu Soke – my second father.

Author's Note: do, *jutsu* or sport?

There is a lot of debate among karate-ka about the differences between sport karate, karate-*jutsu* and karate-*do*. Any of the three may be referred to by the common name: karate.

Sport karate is the participation in tournaments. Sport karate itself is neither good nor bad. Whether it becomes a good or bad experience depends on the attitude of the participant.

Karate-*jutsu* is the art of using karate for fighting. It is about 'effective karate', and what works in a fight situation.

Karate-*do* is the art of using karate as a way of life. It is about developing the individual as a person: to 'seek perfection of character'.

For ease of reading, I use 'karate' throughout this book. However, I try to primarily study and follow the art of karate-*do*.

FOREWORD

When I first saw that Seamus O'Dowd had written a book I was surprised, because I always think of him as being quite young. Sometimes we lose track of time and the years go by more quickly than we realise. Seamus has now been a student of SKIF for thirty years, and I have known him personally for much of that time. I first visited his dojo in Dublin around twenty years ago, and have visited there many times since. He has trained with me not only in Ireland, but in many other countries too. He also has been to Japan for training for extended periods on more than ten occasions.

Although I have known Seamus for many years, he has never stopped learning and growing his karate. Many years ago when I first visited Ireland, long before I knew Seamus, I realised Ireland had poor etiquette. I asked Sensei McCarthy, the first Chairman of SKIF Ireland, to work to educate the students in Ireland, and it greatly improved thereafter. Ireland is now a leading country in showing respect and karate etiquette. Seamus clearly understands the values of correct etiquette, and this has helped him in his study of karate, and on his travels to many dojos around the world. He has great knowledge and is always willing to speak and work with karate-ka who want to learn. I do not hesitate to applaud his eagerness and hunger to grow his personal karate, for as we say, a karate-ka should never stop learning.

When I wrote my autobiography it occurred to me it was not only my story, but also about the people and karate-ka who directly affected me, good and bad. Within this book, I can see how Seamus has also been influenced by people, especially his father, mother and brothers. This I can closely understand too, for family is a strong bond.

I have said many times that in SKIF, the F stands for family. A Karate Story demonstrates this philosophy very well. Through training in karate, Seamus shows that he has not only friends, but also karate family, all over the world. This is the spirit of SKIF, and is very important. I am always happy when I see my students coming together for tournaments or seminars because I know that every time our bonds of family become stronger. From hard training we learn about humility, loyalty, respect and honour. When we train hard together, these characteristics become the basis for our relationship, and this is what makes us family. I hope that this philosophy will remain a core principle of SKIF for many years to come.

Seamus has been a help to SKIF and to me personally by promoting an area of budo training that I consider to be important. Training in my Bo-Jutsu system, and also T'ai Chi, will be a benefit for all karate-ka, because these will help students to reach a deeper understanding of karate and my karate system. All martial arts are connected. For this reason, SKIF has included a Bo-Jutsu and T'ai Chi system and grading syllabus for several years and I recommend that all members of SKIF study both Bo-Jutsu and T'ai Chi as part of their karate training.

I hope that all readers of this book will enjoy it, and will be inspired to train hard in karate, in order to reap the many benefits detailed in these pages.

Kanazawa Hirokazu, Soke
Shotokan Karate-do International Federation
Japan, 21st November 2015

Prologue – 30 Years

One day about ten years ago Sensei Ray Payne was enjoying lunch at the bar of his favourite pub. There was only one other customer – an old man sitting at the opposite side of the bar, having a pint. The old man looked at Sensei Ray. 'Are you still doing that karate stuff?' he called across the bar.

'I am,' replied Sensei Ray with a smile. 'I've been practising now for thirty years. I'm still trying to get good!'

'Thirty years and you still don't know it all?' said the old man thoughtfully, while taking a sip of his pint. 'Well, you must be very slow.'

That dry wit summed up how a lot of people feel about martial artists, and their lack of understanding of what we do and why we do it.

Thirty years seems like a long time. In many countries it is longer than a 'life' sentence in prison. It is longer than an entire career in some professions. And yet, in karate terms we are barely more than beginners after three decades.

The reason for this is because we don't do it in order to know it all, or finish it, or master it. It is something that becomes a part of how we live, like eating food and breathing air. It is no more an achievement to me that I have been practising karate for thirty years than that I have been eating food for forty-six years.

And yet, it is nice to look back over the last thirty years and remember how far I have come, which also helps me realise how far I still have to go.

1. THE BEGINNING

I was born in Dublin on 11 August 1969, and lived there for the first few years of my life, but then my family moved to a small town called Bandon, twenty miles west of Cork City, and that is where I grew up.

I started karate training at the local karate club, but my beginnings were humble, to say the least: actually, I didn't really want to start at all! This was as a result of my earlier experiences as a child. I am one of four sons. Brendan is the eldest; Des is two years younger; I came along another two years later; and finally Enda was born four years after me.

I didn't really like sports as a child. It is only now when I look back that I realise why. Des is an excellent sportsman. He was good at whatever sport or game he played and was always on the first team. Football, hurling, soccer, rugby – you name it. He even played tennis, basketball and badminton, which were considered minority sports where we come from. Being two years younger than him, when he moved up an age group (from under-tens to under-twelves, or under-twelves to under-fourteens), I moved up into his previous group.

The coaches would look at my name and say, 'Great, you're Des' brother,' and put me straight on the team. But I am left-handed, and was not as coordinated (or as talented) as Des. Invariably, after a couple of training sessions, or maybe a match, I would be relegated to the subs bench … of the reserve team! So I dropped out of the various sports one by one, and by my mid teens I was no longer involved in any sports at all.

In the meantime Des decided he wanted to try something a bit different, and convinced Brendan to join the local karate club with him. I used to watch them practising together, but not with any great interest, if I am honest. After a year Des did something unusual for him – he dropped out of the karate club, but Brendan kept going. Actually, Des returned to karate many years later, but for the majority of the timeframe of this book he was not training.

Without Des to work with, Brendan turned to me. He would often ask me to attack him in some way so that he could practise what they had been doing in class. Of course, as a low grade, his control was not as good as it could have been, so I often got bumps and bruises from these practice sessions.

When I turned sixteen in August 1985 my mother told me that she was concerned that I was not involved in any sport or club, and encouraged me to join something. Brendan suggested I give karate a try, so I figured I might as well have a go: after all, if he was going to practise on me, I may as well know how to defend against his attacks!

I

So when the beginners' classes started that October I took Des's old karate-*gi* and white belt and went down to the training venue. Training was held in an old building called The Allen Institute. When I found the men's changing room, I became very shy and self-conscious, probably worried that I was not going to live up to the accomplishments of my brothers yet again. I didn't even know who the instructor was.

There were three people in the changing room, all chatting as though they knew each other. One of the men turned to me and asked if I was starting the beginners' classes.

'Yes,' was my monosyllabic reply. I said nothing more, but started pulling my karate-*gi* out of the bag. The man spoke again when he saw I had a karate-*gi*. 'Have you done karate before?' He asked me.

'No.' Again, my shyness restricted conversation. He gave up, and chatted to the others instead. More and more people came into the changing room, and I was glad to be lost in the crowd.

The Allen Institute had a lot of character. It was an imposing grey building beside the bank of the River Bandon that ran through the heart of the town and gave the town its name. The changing rooms were on the ground floor, but the hall was up a narrow flight of stairs, and it was quite small. There was a rickety trapdoor in the floor near the back of the hall, which all the students tried to avoid, because it was not flush with the rest of the floor and was a bit of a nuisance. People often stubbed their toes on it if they were not careful.

When we went up the stairs and into the training hall there were over fifty beginners, all eager to become the next Bruce Lee. It was very crowded and noisy. There were a few other guys my age that I had seen around at school, so we got talking together before the class started. I finally began to relax a little.

'Who's that over there?' I asked one of them, pointing to the man who had spoken to me in the changing room. My friend laughed. 'That's the boss!' he replied. It turned out that he was Sensei Ray Payne, the instructor at the club. At the time he had just received his 3rd Dan, and already had a great reputation for his karate knowledge and ability.

I paid my £1 for the training and went down near the back of the class, hoping that he wouldn't pick on me for being so rude in the changing room. If I could just get through the class, I would be ok. I could always quit afterwards, I reasoned.

Get through the class? I didn't get thought the warm-up without drawing trouble. All the exercises were strange to me, although I enjoyed them. I found that I was naturally flexible, so the stretches were easier for me than for most of the others. However, near the end of the warm-up we were doing straight-leg stretches – swinging the leg high up in front of us. I was beside the wall, so I put my hand on it for balance as I swung my leg. Big mistake.

'That wall will hold itself up!' roared Sensei Ray, glaring down the hall towards me.

I replied with some smart-ass answer, typical of a teenager. It was something like: 'Are you sure? It looks old to me.'

'What did you say?' Now he was mad. Everyone turned to look at me.

'Nothing. Sorry,' I mumbled, wondering why I had ever come and wishing I could disappear through the trapdoor under my feet. Fortunately for me, he let it go and carried on with the class. But he had made his mark. No more than ten minutes into our first-ever karate session, and we all knew that our sensei was not someone to mess with, and no-one in that class ever tried to get cheeky with him again.

Because there were too many of us for the size of the hall he told us that he would decide by the end of the class who would be allowed to stay, and who would be asked to move to a Saturday morning class, when he taught younger children. At first I figured it wouldn't matter whether I was given permission to stay or not, because I didn't think I would be coming back; but as the class progressed I started to really enjoy myself. For the first time in a sporting activity, I found that being left-handed was not a hindrance but an advantage because we used both sides equally, and my natural flexibility was also useful.

By the time the class finished I had made friends with several of the guys during partner-work drills, which I later learned were called *kumite*. We were anxious to know if we would be able to keep training together. All thoughts of quitting had long since left my mind, and I was already looking forward to the next class, hoping that I would be allowed to stay with this group.

We were lucky. The cut-off age to stay in this class was set at sixteen, and we all just made it into that category. Almost forty of us were allowed to continue training on Tuesday and Thursday evenings. The guys I met in that first class were Greg, Shane, Trevor and Peter, and we were all around the same age. Even though I am the only one still directly involved in karate, I still consider them all friends to this day. Relieved and elated that we had made the grade, we went and changed, and then I snuck back into the hall to watch my brother in the more advanced class.

I was hooked.

2. White Belt

Over the next two years I missed a total of three classes – and felt bad about each one. Every Tuesday and Thursday evening I went training. I also jumped at the chance to attend the rare Friday evening that beginners were invited to the advanced classes.

Sensei Ray was always strict during training. He was (and still is) an inspirational instructor. His classes moved at a fast pace, and we had no choice but to keep up. Having not been involved in other physical activities for some time, I found it tough going.

One day, after watching the advanced class that Brendan was in, I asked him when it starts to get easier.

'It doesn't,' was his reply.

'What do you mean?' I asked, panicking a little.

'As you get fitter, the pace and intensity increases, so you're always kept under pressure.'

I was disheartened at first. I was finding it very tough. But the more I thought about it, the more stubborn I became, and I decided to see it as a challenge. I began working hard on fitness and strength in my own time. Slowly, my athleticism improved, although my brother was absolutely right – it never gets easy.

Strength was another issue for me. I was quite skinny as a teenager, and not naturally strong. I think what I heard most often from Sensei Ray for the first couple of years was 'STRONGER!', which was often bellowed across the hall and aimed directly at me. At that point, because I was quiet and the club was so big, he didn't know my name. In fact, I don't think he even knew that I was Brendan's brother.

We trained for more than seven months before we were allowed to take the first grading examination. At that stage, our numbers had reduced from about forty to twenty-three. The group worked well together and developed strong relationships.

The grading examination was held in Cork City, about twenty miles away. The World Chief Instructor of Shotokan Karate-do International Federation (SKIF), Hirokazu Kanazawa Sensei, came to conduct one of his regular training seminars and grading examinations. We had all heard about the legendary Kanazawa Sensei and, as beginners, were totally in awe of him.

The training and examinations took place in the Mayfield Sports Complex. It was a vast old hall, with cold stone tiles on a concrete floor. It was hardly ideal for karate training, but it was one of the few places that could cope with the numbers of students training at that time.

In our class there were about 200 beginners and white belts, all eagerly awaiting Kanazawa Sensei's arrival. This was the mid

1980s and karate was at the height of its popularity. The training was naturally basic, but I remember how dynamic and powerful Kanazawa Sensei was. More than that, I was amazed by his presence. He didn't have to *do* anything impressive: he exuded strength and his magnetic energy seemed to reverberate throughout the room. I had never experienced anything like it.

Afterwards he sat and patiently signed autographs. Karate suits, books, entry tickets for the seminar – you name it, he signed it. I asked him to sign my copy of his *Basic Karate Katas* book and he naturally obliged. This was the first time that I got close enough to bow to him directly; and I couldn't believe it when he held out his hand to shake mine. Little did I know that in a few years we would develop a lasting relationship.

The grading itself was terrifying. Bear in mind that I had never really achieved anything in any sporting activity. I now found myself in a group of six, with literally hundreds of other students. I was understandably nervous. My group was one of the first out on the floor to perform our basics. I had stage fright with so many people watching, and was sure they were all looking at me. I stood with my mouth open as I went through the motions while performing the first few techniques. Fortunately I quickly forgot about the people watching as I got caught up in the moves we were being asked to perform, and by the time we did our kata at the end of the grading, I felt fairly confident.

My friends and I were given our results together – we all passed. Sensei Ray said that Shane and I nearly earned double gradings, but our basics were too weak at the beginning of the test. We knew we had messed up, but at least we still passed. It felt like a massive achievement. We were white belts!

In our organisation, although as beginners we wore the white belts we received with our suits, it was only after our grading that we officially became 'white belts'. We wore these belts again after the second grading, which was called 'second white belt'. So it was common for students to wear a white belt for more than a year after they started training, but it was a big deal to us to be 'official' white belts, and not just beginners any more.

We did our second white belt grading later the same year. Now there were only eighteen of the original class still remaining, but our group formed a close-knit bond, and we all attended regularly. None of us had a job that summer, so we would meet in the local park most days and do some extra training together. We had a lot of fun working to improve our skills and practising new techniques on each other. We were fanatical about training, often gathering for several hours in the morning, regrouping after lunch and tottering off to the dojo for the evening class. I had karate on the brain: in school I would often respond to teachers with an assertive '*Oss!*' followed by an embarrassed blush.

One day after class, Sensei Ray had taken off his black belt and set it aside. One of the white belts picked it up, took off his belt and cheekily wrapped Sensei Ray's black belt around his waist. Everyone laughed. One of the other white belts had a camera with him, so he got it out and took a picture. Then several others wanted their picture taken wearing the black belt. While everyone was taking it in good spirits, I had a nagging doubt about whether it was the right thing to do or not, and when Shane was offered the belt, he put words to my concerns.

'No thanks,' he said. 'I haven't earned the right to wear that belt.'

'Come on,' replied one of the others. 'It might be the only chance we ever get to wear a black belt.'

If I had doubts initially, that statement convinced me not to do it. It was defeatist. No way was I putting on a belt I had not earned, and no way was I admitting that I might not ever get to earn a black belt of my own. Shane and I were the only two who refused to wear that belt: in fact, neither of us ever wore a belt that we had not earned.

Greg, one of my close friends from that group, found a copy of Kanazawa Sensei's video of Kanku-Dai (a black-belt kata). Although we had only learned two katas so far in class, we started trying to learn Kanku-Dai from the video. We spent hours trying to follow it in Greg's sitting room, looking over our shoulders at the screen and adjusting the furniture. It took a while, but we eventually had a working knowledge of the kata, although we didn't dare tell Sensei Ray! After all, we were still only white belts...

3. COMPETITION

In the autumn of 1986 we were told that the national championships would be taking place shortly. Sensei told us that not everyone would be allowed to enter, and that he would select students for each category of the event. Even though we had now been training for a year, we were still in the white belt category. Training became more focused on competition fighting and on kata. We were told the rules, and held practice fights in class.

Shane and I loved partnering together and used to have some good fights. On the Thursday night before the national championships we had a particularly good one. Shane caught me perfectly with a couple of jabs and reverse punches, as well as a good mawashi-geri (roundhouse kick). We both liked that technique, and I returned the compliment with one of my own; and I also managed to sweep his front leg as he attacked, catching him with a reverse punch as he lost balance. Sensei Ray had been going around observing all the students, and each time one of us pulled off a good technique he just happened to be watching. That was our last training session before the competition, and still none of the white belts had been told whether he or she could compete or not. By this stage we felt we must not have been selected, because we didn't have any more classes to prepare.

The following evening I went to watch the advanced class. I sat shivering with a mix of cold and adrenalin, watching the great training and wishing I could take part. At the end of class Sensei Ray announced who was permitted to compete in the championships, and who would fight on the team. Surprisingly, he also said he had selected two white belts, and named Shane and me – after a year of training it was the first time I had heard him actually say my name! I was delighted to have been picked.

Most of the people in the advanced class were competing, but as only two white belts had been chosen, there were a few disappointed people from our class that weekend. To their credit, they all travelled with us on the bus to support the club. There was a great atmosphere as we headed up the country early on Sunday morning.

By the time we arrived at the venue, large crowds had gathered. The children's events ran first, so we were waiting around for hours before anything really got going. We were particularly eager for the men's black belt kata event, as Sensei Ray had been champion for the previous few years and we were willing him to retain his title.

Before that, the men's white belt kata event was announced. Shane and I went to the arena and lined up with at least fifty other competitors. Shane was unlucky to be beaten in the third round,

7

but I somehow managed to keep going. After the fourth round our numbers had been whittled down to four, and the referee announced that we made it to the final, which would be held later in the day. I was in shock. I couldn't believe it – all my friends congratulated me on doing so well, but my sense of elation didn't last very long as Sensei Ray immediately brought me back to Earth with a bang.

'You haven't won anything yet,' he reminded me. 'I want you to win it now. Second place won't do.'

'*Oss!*' I responded, bowing. 'What kata should I do?'

'Do you know Heian Yondan?' he asked me.

I was surprised that he was suggesting this kata. I did know it, sort of, but it was the fourth kata – an advanced kata for white belts. I told him I wasn't sure of it. He thought about it for a minute and then took me aside and worked on it a few times. He wanted me to do it because my kicks were good.

Before the kata final we had the sparring event. Shane fought well, and was narrowly beaten again in the third round. I thought I had scored with a roundhouse kick in the first round but the judges didn't award it. Instead, they gave a half point to my opponent for the punch with which he followed up. I was annoyed, and it cost me. I wasn't concentrating when the match restarted and my opponent stepped in with a simple reverse punch for another half point. Match over.

I was gutted to have done so poorly, especially considering I had been selected because of my sparring in the dojo. The kata finals would have to be my redeeming grace.

Four of us from the dojo made the finals: me in the white belt section; one in the intermediate sparring; one in the brown belt kata; and Sensei Ray in the black belt kata. Sensei Ray brought the finalists together for a chat just before the finals started. He told us that he wanted at least three first places from the four of us – no pressure then!

My final was on first. Each finalist performed their kata, after which the judges gave their scores. I did Heian Yondan as my sensei had instructed, and tied for first place with one of the others. The judges had us come out together to decide the winner and made us do Heian Shodan (the first kata) again, and at the end, all judges raised white flags. I had won. It was my first sporting victory.

My friend in the intermediate sparring final also won his event, but the guy in the brown belt kata came third. Sensei Ray won his event with an amazing kata, so we had met his three-titles target. I had never even won so much as a participation medal in school, so I was delighted that my first ever trophy was for national champion, even if it was only a white belt event.

It was late that night when we returned home. I placed my trophy on the kitchen table for my parents to see when they got up. When I came down the next morning, my father was eating his breakfast.

The trophy had been moved off the table, and not a word was said. This was typical of him – a man of few words.

Funnily enough, a few years later a friend of my father's was visiting the house and I was left to entertain him for a few minutes while my father finished a phone call. After I poured the man a drink, we started to make small talk. He asked me if I was the one who did karate, so I pointed out that three of us did karate. But he persisted, saying that one of us kept winning all these trophies, and listed off several of my achievements. I was embarrassed and asked him how he knew all of this. I was stunned when he told me that my father 'never shuts up about it'. He never uttered a word to us directly, but it seemed he was vocal enough when he wanted to be.

National Championships 1986 (White Belt Kata event)

9

4. INSPIRATION

Back in the dojo after the competition the only thing that changed was that Sensei Ray now knew my name, so now he could yell 'Stronger, Seamus!', just in case there was any doubt about who he was unhappy with.

Brendan and I used to practise in the kitchen at home. The oven was at the perfect height to act as a mirror for us to check our techniques, so we often worked on kata or kicks there. One day I was sitting at the kitchen table, watching Brendan working on the kata for his next grading. He was doing Tekki-Shodan in preparation for his brown belt test. I gaped at him, mesmerised by the kata and wondering how he could perform such complicated moves. I remembered that I had struggled with learning the turns in Heian Shodan, so if I found such a basic kata difficult, how would I ever be able to do this one?

As I watched, full of admiration for Brendan's kata, I resigned myself to my fate. Maybe I'll be able to get as far as purple belt before I have to give up, I thought, because I'll never learn that kata. But shortly afterwards something happened to make me want to try to go further than I had thought would be possible.

Brendan was allowed to train in the advanced class on Friday nights, so I used to go along to watch. It was traditional for the class to go for a couple of drinks after training on Fridays and I used to tag along, just because I was there. I was only seventeen. I didn't drink and was always broke so I often didn't even have enough money for lemonade. I was also very shy, so I rarely said a word. I just loved the atmosphere, and listening to the various karate stories. It was nice to be involved, however modestly, in these social events.

One evening shortly after the national championships we were sitting in the pub chatting as usual: well, as per usual, the others were chatting while I sat and listened. Soon people started talking about the recent national championships, and how dominant our sensei was in the men's kata event. One of the black belts asked him if he felt anyone could claim his title in the coming years. Everyone was immediately interested to hear his answer, so the group went quiet and listened expectantly. Sensei paused for a few moments before he answered. Then he pointed out that he was a semi-professional instructor; he mused that it was not really fair to compare him with the others in his category as they didn't have such readily available facilities to train. He also doubted that there would be anyone to challenge his standard for some time.

Then one of the brown belts asked him who would take over his kata title when he eventually retired from competing. At first, he wouldn't answer. Students asked if it would be the guy who was runner-up at the nationals, and he shook his head. Then they asked about some of the other prominent competitors, including some of the junior black belts, but again he said no. By now everyone was intrigued, and then he really confused us all by saying that he knew who would be the next person to dominate the men's black belt kata title after him; and that person was among the fifteen or so people who sat there with him.

We all looked around, wondering which of the brown or black belts in the group he meant.

Then he pointed at me, the most junior person in the group. Everyone was stunned. Some of them didn't even know my name, or if they did it was only from hearing Sensei Ray yelling at me to be stronger. I felt my face burning as I went puce. I wanted to disappear. He must have made a mistake, or gone crazy – possibly both!

'If Seamus keeps training, he will be the one to take over my title,' he said calmly.

The rest of the guys cast sidelong glances at me for the rest of the evening. I couldn't get it out of my head. I was convinced he had lost his mind. In fact, to this day I still do not understand how he could have made such a statement, or what capabilities he could have seen in me at that time. After all, I was only a white belt, and there were plenty of other karate-*ka* in our dojo and across the country who had much better kata than me. Over the next few days and weeks I became determined to fulfil his prediction. I convinced myself I would not quit; that I would train as hard as I could; and I would live up to his expectations in me. It was a strange and bold statement for an instructor to make about such a junior student, but I believe that it had a profound influence on the rest of my life. I consider that statement to be one of the main reasons I kept training, even after all my friends dropped out, one by one.

By this time, the SKIF European Championships were fast approaching. Normally this would not mean anything to such junior students, but that particular year they were held in Cork, very close to where we lived. A large group from our dojo went to watch with a mixture of eager anticipation and jealousy. Perhaps, more importantly, we knew Sensei Ray and several others on the Irish team and we wanted to show a united front for the home team.

It was wonderful to be a spectator: the competitors' standard was exceptional, and our group of spectators was enthralled. Sensei Ray became SKIF European Kata Champion that day, and there were several other Irish medal winners also. We all secretly dreamed of one day making the Irish team and getting to represent our country, though none of us would admit to it because it seemed impossible. I never forgot the experience of watching the international competitors that day. As I progressed through my karate training, the impossible dream slowly became a steadfast plan.

5. Coloured Belt

Our training varied week on week. Although we followed the syllabus for grading examinations, we also learned more advanced and unusual techniques. We were never really told which techniques were standard learning for our grading syllabus, and which were more advanced. Sensei Ray often had a general class where everyone, from white to black belts, was invited. Oftentimes, the lower grades performed the black belt combinations along with everyone else. While it was a challenge in class, we were more than prepared when the time came to grade.

Our third grading examination was now approaching, approximately fifteen months after we started training. Twelve of our original class of forty remained. Of course, there was now a new batch of beginners in the dojo, so we were no longer the most junior students. We were excited about this grading because it would mean getting rid of the white belts and finally having a yellow 'coloured' belt, assuming we passed. The grading examination was to be conducted by Sensei George Reilly, the chief instructor for Ireland at that time, and he had a reputation for being a very tough examiner.

The training seminar before the examination revealed him to be an excellent technician, and hard as nails. He was a perfectionist, making us repeat techniques over and over until he was satisfied that we understood what he wanted us to do. It was good training, but my mind was focused on the examination ahead, so it was difficult to concentrate on the class itself. The butterflies were already in full flight in my stomach.

As usual we were called out in groups of six for the examination. In our group, my name was called first. That meant that I stood closest to the examiner, facing sideways. Shane was last called in our group. I was disappointed that we were separated: we had become great friends, were often partnered together, and had worked hard in preparation for our exam. I was immediately put on the back foot. The examination would be a little more difficult partnered with someone else.

First we were asked to do several basic techniques up and down the floor. We were surprised that we were not asked some of the more complicated combinations that we had been doing in the dojo for the previous couple of months, but we performed what we were asked to do to the best of our ability.

Next was the kumite (partner work). I was paired with a guy who was a good bit older than me. Again, we were closest to the examiner, with each pair of students standing progressively further away. My partner was very strong, but a bit clumsy. I knew him well enough to remember to be sharp with my blocking. It seemed to work well, though my arms were sore and bruised by the end of it.

Finally, we had kata – Heian Nidan. I liked this kata because it had kicks in it and I was flexible enough to be able to kick high. All I remember about performing the kata is that I was still cursing my kumite partner because my forearms were throbbing from blocking his iron-bar arms earlier.

When the kata finished there was silence apart from our heavy breathing. The chief instructor and Sensei Ray were seated at the table doing the paperwork and marking our examination records. After what seemed like an eternity, the examiner pointed his pen at me and said something. I wasn't expecting him to be talking to me, so I didn't catch what he said.

'Do you want to try for a double grading?' he repeated, somewhat impatiently. I didn't know what to say. I didn't know what trying for a double grading would entail. I was trying to figure out why he was asking me and not Shane, because I considered Shane to have better karate than me. I was obviously taking too long to answer, so Sensei Ray asked me the question again. I knew this was not a good sign, and that I should have answered decisively the first time I was asked.

'Oss!' I said, as loudly and confidently as I could, though I suspect it sounded rather shaky.

'Ok,' said the examiner. 'Do you know Heian Sandan?'

'Oss!' I replied, a little stronger this time. I knew this kata. I could perform all five Heian kata (plus Kanku-Dai, but that was still a secret!). They might not have been to any particular standard, but I could do them.

I was the only one invited to try for a double grading. As I did the kata, my mind was racing. I was trying to do it strong, because I knew that my lack of physical power was my key weakness, but at the same time I was trying to figure out why I was being given the opportunity when others were not. By the time I gave a loud *kiai* (shout) at the end of the kata, I had figured it was simply because I was closest to the examiner, and Shane was furthest away. He could see me more easily.

When the results of all the examinations were announced, my friends were awarded 7th Kyu – yellow belts – and I was awarded 6th Kyu – green belt. Everyone congratulated me on getting the double grading, but I felt guilty. I even told Shane that he would have been the one to get it had our positions in the line been switched. He didn't seem to mind though, and was genuinely happy for me, which I greatly appreciated.

As coloured belts, we were now able to train in the more advanced class that my brother was in on Tuesdays and Thursdays, and we were able to attend on Fridays as well. I would finally be able to participate in the class I had spent hours watching.

On the first night in the dojo after the grading we were all proudly wearing our brand-new belts. Being the only one who received a double grading, I was probably prouder than anyone, but pride comes before a fall... During class we did a lot of partner work and changed partners regularly. After a while, one of my partners pointed towards my belt. I just had a silly grin on my face, thinking they were pointing out my nice new belt.

Then we changed partners, and my next partner also pointed to my belt. I grinned again. Wow, my new belt was getting a lot of attention. Then my partner pointed at it again.

'Nice, isn't it?' I whispered.

'No, you idiot,' she hissed at me. 'The knot is undone!'

I looked down to see the belt was nearly falling off. Unlike my old white belt, the new belt was stiff so the knot didn't want to stay in place. It had loosened so much that it had come undone and I was too preoccupied and proud to notice. Idiot indeed. I blushed and sheepishly re-tied it.

As my brother had pointed out to me much earlier, the training never got easier – it just became more intense as we moved up the grades. We immediately noticed that Sensei Ray's expectations had changed: the classes were longer and more frequent; the intensity was higher; and as always, there was a lot to absorb. We learned how to understand and manipulate our bodies to make better use of certain techniques. In many ways the training became more physical, and applicable to everyday uses.

One evening in class, Sensei Ray was not happy with our partner work. He started shouting at us to attack stronger and harder. We still were not doing it right and he became frustrated, so he sat us all down in a circle. Then he made me stand in front of him.

'You are all going too easy on your partners,' he explained. 'You might think you are being nice to your friend by going easy on them, but you are not. We are here to learn how to block attacks. How can we learn whether our block works or not, if the attack is not realistic? If you are too far away, your partner does not have to block. If you move your attack away at the last moment, your partner does not get the feel of the block working. If you do not attack with speed and power, then your partner will not learn to use speed and power to block. The way you attack is the way your partner will defend.'

We all nodded, and said 'Oss!' Sensei made a lot of sense with this little speech. Then he faced me and continued.

'If I am partnered with Seamus, I owe it to him to attack strong. If he is my friend – and he is – then I must work hard to help him improve his karate. Then he must do the same for me.'

This was the first time that Sensei Ray called me a friend. I had never thought about it like that until then. I had no time to dwell on the significance of what that meant, because he immediately announced his attack. We had been doing three-step training, with three different attacks one after the other. As he launched his first attack my instincts took over and I moved back and blocked faster than I had ever moved before. Almost as soon as I had blocked that, the second attack was coming at me. I blocked again, just about moving in time. Then the third attack – front kick – came at me. My arm flew down to block it as I frantically stepped back out of the way. Before I knew what was happening, my counter-attack flew out with the same intensity as his attacks had been. I had never realised I could move so fast, until he gave me no choice: I either moved and blocked, or I would have been hit, albeit with control.

That lesson made a lasting impression on me, and on everyone else, because our partner work was far more intense and realistic for the rest of that class, and for every other class. It is a lesson I have carried throughout my karate career.

6. JUSTICE

I loved training as a green belt. In fact, I consider the period from green belt to purple belt to be one of my 'golden' periods of training. In karate, people sometimes talk about the 'golden age' of karate, where the first generation of instructors travelled from Japan like missionaries to bring karate to the world. Since then, people have used the phrase sometimes to refer to highlights in their own training. When I earned my green belt, I felt as if a world of opportunity had opened to me. I learned a lot, and it was all very exciting. I was now able to train in all the classes at our dojo (the more the merrier!). Our younger brother Enda had also joined the dojo, so there were three brothers actively training in the club. Along with several other students, I would go and train in the white belt class for the first hour, and then in our intermediate class for another hour and a half on Tuesdays and Thursdays, and then I got to train in the coveted Friday night advanced classes too.

One of the newer students was a keyholder for the town hall, so a group of us often went there at weekends, when it was not in use, to do a bit of extra training. Another green belt in the club, Daniel, used to do Tae-Kwon-Do, and he had a friend who was preparing for his black belt in that art. He came along for a bit of extra training with us one day. After we showed each other the types of basics and katas we each did, he suggested a bit of sparring. I readily agreed, and we bowed to each other. He started off with a lot of high-spinning kicks from a long way out so I was easily able to avoid them. When he got in a bit closer, I simply ducked under a high kick, and punched him in the stomach.

'Hey! You can't do that!' he complained.

'Why not?' I asked, genuinely surprised.

'That's not how we spar,' he said.

'Well,' I reasoned, 'it is how we spar, and we are here to learn from each other, right?'

He agreed, and we ended up having a good session where we learned from each other's differences, rather than trying to force ourselves to be the same.

We participated in a couple of inter-club competitions around that time. I was successful in the kata competitions, but I still struggled with the sparring events. Although my sparring in the dojo was good, I struggled to translate my skills into points at these events. Most of the people who did well at our level just stuck with reverse punch, but I preferred to kick. That meant that I was often a sitting duck for a counterpunch when my opponent blocked my kicks. Still, I was gathering quite a collection of kata trophies, with their little plastic men doing a side-kick on top.

When the regional (Munster) championships came around I was 5th Kyu, which we called 1st purple belt (in some groups they called it blue belt). Shane had double-graded to catch up with me again, which I was glad about. The championships were being held in my home town that year, and I was hoping that my parents would come and watch, as they had never attended any of our previous events. I was in a category with 7th Kyu (yellow belt) to 4th Kyu (2nd purple belt). Unfortunately, this event was held earlier than I expected, and my parents had not arrived by the time the elimination rounds were completed. I got to the kata final, which would be held later in the evening.

Sensei Ray spoke to me and told me that I couldn't do Heian Yondan anymore, because now it was a kata below my grade. He wanted me to keep doing higher-level katas. By now he knew that I was able to do Kanku-Dai, so he told me to do that in the final. It was audacious for a 5th Kyu to do such a kata, but he knew best and I did as I was told.

My parents arrived and watched some of the events, but the finals are always held at the end of the day, so they had left again before my final event. Nevertheless, I managed to win with Kanku-Dai, and I was delighted to win it because it was such a difficult and long kata to perform.

That was the closest that my parents got to watching any karate for a long time. In fact, my father only once ever came to a class, years later in Dublin when I was teaching. It wasn't that they weren't interested, but they didn't really understand the art or the level of commitment needed. My father was impressed when he did come to watch that class, and that was good enough for me.

The national championships came around again while I was still 5th Kyu. The organisers changed the categories for the competition that year: 5th Kyu to 1st Kyu (purple belts and brown belts) were now in one category. That meant that I was the lowest grade possible for our section, and most of the other competitors were brown belts with at least one or two years of additional experience. This put me at a big disadvantage before we had even started.

That year's competition took place in a small town hall in Killarney. The space was cramped with karate-*ka*, all fuelled with adrenalin. Two arenas were placed in the main floor space. The large stage area had been cleared and matted to make a third.

Our kata event took place on the stage. The referee was Sensei McCarthy, and the two judges were guys I didn't know. I was called out in the first round against a brown belt. I didn't fancy my chances much and made the mistake that many people make – I looked at the belt instead of the person.

The referee selected a kata for us to perform: Heian Yondan. My favourite! I was pleased. Maybe I had a chance after all. We did the kata, and the referee blew his whistle for the two judges and himself to raise their flags. I couldn't see the two judges because they sit behind the competitors, but the referee was in front. He raised a white flag for me. Then I saw him shaking his head. He put down his flag and then raised both flags crossed, indicating a draw. Apparently, the two judges behind had both raised red flags for the other competitor, but the referee overruled them. We would have to go again.

He selected a second kata. Heian Sandan. We both did the kata again, and again the same thing happened. The referee raised his flag for me, and the other two raised their flags for the other competitor. The referee brought them both up to speak to them. He was clearly not happy with them. When they sat down again he raised both flags crossed once more. Another draw.

After the third kata, when the same thing happened, the referee called for the chief referee to come to the arena. Sensei McCarthy explained what was happening. The chief referee made us perform Heian Shodan, the most basic kata: he refereed us by himself, relieving all the others for this one kata. We had barely finished when he raised a white flag for me. He then told the two judges that they were disqualified from judging for the rest of the day. Two different judges were appointed to assist the referee for the rest of the event.

My fellow competitor came over to me to apologise. 'I could see your kata was better than mine,' he told me. 'I am sorry.' We shook hands with no hard feelings. It wasn't his fault. He was only on the floor competing. Someone told me later that the two judges were from the same dojo as my competitor, but I don't know if that was true.

I made it all the way to the final and was joined by Shane and two brown belts from our dojo. One of our brown belts, a 1st Kyu, won the event, and I was runner-up. It was the first time that I had lost a kata competition, but I didn't mind because it was to a fellow team-mate and friend. Given the way the category was set anyway, I would have gladly taken second place at the beginning of the day, and for a while it looked like I wasn't getting past the first round! I was certainly grateful that Sensei McCarthy refused to allow what was apparently an injustice.

There were several other tournaments while I was a purple belt, but for each of them the brown belts were in a different category, so I didn't have to contend with them. A friendly rivalry developed between myself and a guy called Adrian, who was from a club in Cork City. He and I often reached the final of the kata events together, and we got to know each other. Although we were competitive on the floor, we greeted each other as friends and shared a few laughs off the floor. There was a sense of camaraderie because we were often in similar circumstances with competition. I got to know people from various groups at the different tournaments; it felt good to know karate could bring people together, even if they were adversaries for a short while.

My training became slightly disrupted around this time as school exams loomed closer. Greg, Trevor and Peter had dropped out by now, as had some of our other friends, so I didn't have as many people to train with outside of class. Shane and I were still there, and about five others from the original class. Shane was able to train more than me at that time, and because he did a grading examination that I missed, he was now a grade ahead.

I tried to make up for missing some training by reading books on karate when I could. I had received my first martial arts book, *The Zen Way to the Martial Arts*, from Brendan when I was still a white belt. There were not so many martial arts books available in those days, and it certainly was not so easy to find them. I was fascinated. Sensei Ray recommended two books when I asked him about what I should read. They were *Moving Zen* by C.W. Nicol and *Spirit of the Empty Hand* by Stan Schmidt. Once read, they inspired and motivated me to keep training, even when my friends had quit and life commitments seemed to get in the way. I dreamed of becoming a black belt. I dreamed of going to Japan to train, and I wondered if such dreams could ever come true.

People sometimes get fixated on gradings and belts, but we were learning that it was more important to focus on good training. In doing that, the belts and grades sorted themselves out over time. Shane and I started together and earned our first two grades together. Then I went a grade ahead of him, and then he caught up with me the next time. Then he went a grade ahead of me. He was now first brown belt, testing for second brown, while I was second purple belt preparing to test for first brown.

Once the school exams were over I was able to refocus on training. In preparing for brown belt I had to work on the kata that I thought I would never be able to learn: Tekki-Shodan. It turned out that I liked the kata, mostly because my kiba-dachi (horse stance) was good, but also because I liked the sharp hand movements once I got used to them.

Kanazawa Sensei conducted the tests again. This was my fourth time testing directly with him. He must have liked my kata (and everything else) because he gave me my second double grading so I skipped first brown belt and went straight to second brown belt. In doing so I had caught back up with Shane, who earned his second brown belt the same day. On the way home after that examination, I remember smiling at the irony that I used to think that I would never be able to get to brown belt, yet it turned out to be one of the best tests I had done. Perhaps I was too quick to set limits for myself.

7. Becoming a Black Belt

The club was becoming bigger, with a lot of brown and black belts, so Sensei Ray decided to devote Friday-night training to brown and black belts only. That suited us fine, because it meant that the training was more advanced. We started learning a lot more of the black belt kata, and doing a lot of semi-freestyle training.

Nijushiho became my favourite kata. It suited me well, being a very technical kata with flowing smooth movements and two side-kicks, and I was encouraged by Sensei Ray to use this kata for competitions from then on. And then the first time I did it in a kata final, Adrian beat me into second place. He was delighted, as it was the first time he had done that. Of course I was disappointed to lose, but Adrian was a very nice guy, so it was hard not to be happy for him at the same time. I reversed the result when the next opportunity rose, so all was well.

As a brown belt, I also reached the semi-final of a sparring competition, but did not get to the final. At least I was showing that I was not just a kata competitor. However, I did have one success in a sparring competition – in the team event, but not for my own club.

Sensei Timmy Harte used to run an invitational international competition every year, with clubs usually coming from England, Scotland and Wales, as well as Ireland. We were competing in it one time when I was a brown belt. Sensei Ray was talking to Paul Duffy from Dublin, who told him that only four of them had travelled from Dublin that day, so they were one man short to enter the team sparring event. He asked our sensei if he could spare a man to make up a team.

Sensei Ray had his five-man team, and Shane was his sub. I was (at best) his number seven, so he asked me if I wanted to fight with the guys from Dublin. Although I didn't want to be disloyal to my own club, I wanted the experience of more fighting. Also, the four from Dublin were all very experienced international fighters: Paul Duffy, Alan Campbell, Larry Hand and Paul Byrne. Paul Duffy had won a bronze medal at the European Championships in Cork a couple of years earlier and he and Alan Campbell had won the national title several times between them. I readily agreed to make up the numbers on their team. Their strategy was simple enough. They put their best two fighters out first and third, with the weakest fighter (me) in between. Then the other guys brought up the rear. I was told to try and get a draw in my fights, and they would get the wins.

All went to plan in the first round. Duffy went first and won easily. I went out next and went a half point down in the first thirty seconds, getting caught as I tried to kick. When we restarted the fight, I could hear the guys all telling me to just use my hands. I struggled for a while, with no scores for either of us. Then, near the end of the fight, I lifted my knee to pretend to kick. My opponent went to block it, but instead I switched and caught him with a simple reverse punch. *Wazari!* (half point). The match finished a draw, and at least I played an active role, for the first round anyway. The next three fighters duly reeled off wins, so we went through to the second round easily.

In the next round I was not able to score, but I also prevented my opponent from scoring, so it was another draw. We won that round 3-0 though, so my new teammates were happy enough.

Even though I was far less experienced than the others on the team, I felt that they were doing all the real work, and I wanted to try to contribute more. I was determined to try for more than just a draw in the next round. I fought very hard against a tough black belt opponent from Wales. These guys were used to a bit more contact than we usually had; one of their previous rounds had been a bit of a bloodbath, but they were warned by the chief referee and they were more muted when they fought us. I tried for the first minute and a half to fight the way the guys were telling me – keeping my feet on the floor and just working the hands – but I was getting nowhere. There was still no score for either of us with about twenty seconds to go, so I tried to switch strategy and use my kicks. My opponent was caught by surprise, and I was almost quick enough with my roundhouse kick, but he just moved his head back enough at the last instant, and my toe grazed his nose. No score. My teammates were screaming at me not to kick again, because they were afraid I would lose the fight, so I reverted back to plan A, and the fight ended scoreless. Nonetheless, the others on the team did their job, and we were through to the final.

We had some time before the final, so they took me for a bit of coaching, showing me their footwork and telling me how to read an opponent's movement in order to time an attack. I told them that I felt bad because I had not won any of my fights and had not really contributed. They reminded me that they could not have entered the event without me, and that I was doing the job I was assigned. They also pointed out that I had not lost any fights either. They really took me under their wing and made me feel part of the team.

When the final came around, Duffy went out first as usual. He dispatched his opponent without fuss. Then it was my turn. They had been telling me all day to keep my feet on the floor and just use my hands, but I had watched my opponent at other competitions, and I knew he was susceptible to getting caught with a roundhouse kick. I intended to stick to the plan and try to score with punching. But immediately after our first fruitless exchange I saw my opponent's hands drop momentarily. Almost before I realised it, my left leg launched a roundhouse kick and my foot smacked him on the cheek. The referee raised his arm straight up in the air. *Ippon!* A full point and I had won my fight. Our next fighter won also, so we were 3-0 up and had the tournament won.

My teammates joked with me about not using my hands, but they were delighted that I had won my fight. They understood how important it was to me to compete on their team, but also, that I was able to compete, and win, in a way that I found comfortable. When the trophies were being presented, Paul Duffy, the captain, insisted that I lead them to the presentation and receive the trophy, which I thought was a nice touch.

A couple of the guys from my home dojo commented that they would have refused to fight for another dojo, but Sensei Ray defended me by saying that it was great experience, and that it was good for our dojo that I had been on the winning team. Personally speaking, it was just nice to win a trophy that wasn't for kata for a change. The experience really afforded me an opportunity to step up my game, and see what was needed for black-belt standard. I also earned the respect and friendship of these seasoned international fighters. Every experience was helping towards the goal of becoming a black belt.

Sensei Ray is a firm believer that those preparing for black belt should be involved in teaching classes. He used to have a children's class on Saturday mornings, so I was sometimes invited to go along and help him with that. Then one day he told me that one of the other black belts was starting a little dojo in a village a few miles outside Bandon, and asked me if I would go along and help him. On the first night more than ninety adult beginners showed up for training! We split the class between us, and I got my first real taste of teaching students by myself. I helped him for a few months until the numbers naturally declined to a level where the black belt could manage the class numbers single-handed.

Brendan's training was sporadic while he was in college, after which he moved to Limerick for work, but there were no karate clubs near him. He started training in different arts, including judo and Tang-Soo-Do, but it meant that he did not grade in karate for a few years and was stuck on second brown belt. I ended up overtaking him when I got my third brown belt, and then it was time to really focus on the big one – the black-belt test.

Shane and I trained at each and every opportunity we got. We were the only two left from our original class. There was a third student in the club, Mark, also preparing for black belt. He had started the year before us, but now we would be testing together, under Kanazawa Sensei. We had all trained and tested with Kanazawa Sensei several times before. His power, energy and sheer presence were incredible, and he was an inspiring instructor. I particularly loved the way he broke techniques down into their components and explained everything in such detail. It suited the way my brain worked, so I always got a lot out of his classes.

We had three days of training with him before the actual grading, which was held on Sunday morning. I didn't sleep much the night before: my mind was restless, and I meticulously rehearsed the different sections of the syllabus in my mind, hoping I had done enough. I even jumped out of bed a few times to practise a couple of techniques. I was fuelled with a bubbling nervous energy.

All the students got to the dojo early and had warmed up before Kanazawa Sensei arrived. We could tell he was in a serious mood that morning. There were no smiles or jokes – it was straight down to business. He took the examinations very seriously. I had heard stories of the pile of paperwork of those who failed being a lot bigger than that of those who passed, and I began to wonder on which pile my paperwork would end up that day.

Twenty-three students were testing for Shodan (1st Dan) that morning, plus a few others for Nidan (2nd Dan). We were called out in groups of six for the basics first. As fate would have it, Adrian – my rival and friend from kata competitions – was beside me for the basics, and Shane and Mark from my dojo were in the same group. Although Kanazawa Sensei had somewhat impatiently given corrections to the previous group on the floor, fortunately he didn't seem to have as many problems with our group.

When we sat down after the basics while the next groups went out, Adrian and I spoke about the upcoming partner work. We knew we would be partnered together from the way we were out for basics. Not for the first time I was a little disappointed that I would not partner Shane for a grading, but I knew Adrian had a very good standard and it would be fine. We discussed which defences we had prepared so that we would not catch each other unawares. For one of the attacks, the back kick, one of the prescribed defences involves catching the leg and lifting the opponent, throwing them to the floor. We both agreed not to do that one, in case we injured each other and would not be able to finish the examination.

Our group was called out and, as expected, Adrian and I were paired together. I attacked first. We were always told to attack hard but fair, so I attacked with strong spirit and good control. Adrian did all the defences he had said he would, and did them very well. Then it was my turn to defend. Adrian attacked strong also, and there was a lot of positive energy between us. We were really getting stuck in. When it came to his back kick attack, I was so hyped and running on adrenalin that I never thought about the agreement not to throw each other. In fact, I didn't think anything at all – I just reacted. Before I realised what I was doing, I had caught Adrian's leg and lifted him high in the air. As I was dumping him I remembered to control his fall and held him just before he hit the ground. Adrian looked shocked for a second, because he wasn't expecting it, but he gave me a quick grin and a wink as he stood up. He knew it was a good technique, and he knew that we had both done well in a tricky part of the examination. As we walked off the floor I whispered my apologies. He laughed it off and told me not to worry about it, which was typical of his good nature.

We still had our kata to do, but we had to wait for the other groups to do their partner work first. Anyone who has done grading examinations or tournaments knows that the constant stop-start makes it difficult to keep the body adequately warmed up as adrenalin smoulders under the surface, but a bigger problem is maintaining focus and keeping the brain switched on in situations like that. Some of the people on the floor seemed to have lost their focus and were making silly errors. Kanazawa Sensei was getting visibly irked, and we started to worry that he might just fail everyone.

That was out of our hands. All we could do was to keep focused and do the best katas we could. Our group had all chosen Bassai-Dai as our first kata. I don't remember anything from the beginning until I shouted my *kiai* at the last move. I generally consider it a good sign if I can't remember performing my kata, because it means that I did it in a state of *mushin* (the concept of 'no mind' – not thinking, but letting it happen). Of course, this is a different thing to not being able to remember the kata at all. Drawing a blank is not the same as *mushin*!

Kanazawa Sensei chose our second kata – Heian Shodan. A basic kata, but this must not be confused with being easy. There is nowhere to hide or bluff in this kata. Everything must be correct. When it was over, we were dismissed without comment and the other groups were then brought out for their katas. Our test was over, and we could do no more but wait for the results to be announced.

Usually the results are announced immediately after the Dan grade examinations, but this time Kanazawa Sensei said he needed more time to consider and reflect, as he was unhappy with the standard. He said he would announce the results after doing the Kyu gradings. This meant further torture for us, having to wait three or four more hours for the results. However, we made the most of it by offering support to the people in our clubs who were taking part in their own examinations, and the time went quickly enough. After the Kyu examinations were over, all the candidates for the Dan exams were hanging around expectantly, but Kanazawa Sensei still had not made up his mind. He announced that he was going to take the papers back to his hotel and study them again, and that he would give the results at his hotel that evening at 6 pm.

We were disheartened about having to wait, and, not being able to hang around all day, decided to leave. Adrian was from the city, and

25

volunteered to go to the hotel that evening. I gave him my number and asked him to call me when he knew the results. I then got Shane's and Mark's numbers and promised that I would ring them in turn. There were no mobile phones in those days...

It was after 7pm when the phone eventually rang. Adrian told me that I had passed. I breathed a huge sigh of relief, while he went on to say that Shane and Mark had passed too, as had Adrian himself. However, of the twenty-three who tested, only seven passed outright. Six more students had a deferred pass (automatic pass, but deferred for between three months and six months for the student to improve one or two areas), and ten had failed. They would have to take the test again the next time. I congratulated Adrian, and then I rang Shane and Mark to tell them the good news.

It was a shame that we did not get to hear it with a formal announcement in front of everyone, and it was a bit of an anti-climax to be told over the phone, but it didn't really matter. We were black belts, and we felt we had certainly earned them that day. In any case, I got lucky the next day, because I had to go back to Cork City for college, and I happened to meet Kanazawa Sensei out for a walk with some of the senior members of the organisation. One of them recognised me and called me over to say hello to Kanazawa Sensei, and he remembered me from the previous day and congratulated me on passing my grading.

Shane and I had started on the same day, frequently partnered together in class, and came up through the grades together. It was fitting that we got our black belts together. We were the only two out of the original class of forty students that made it to black belt. We were also the only two that had refused to wear Sensei Ray's black belt after class all those years ago. Was it just a coincidence? Maybe it was. Or maybe it showed that our attitudes as white belts differed to that of our peers: we were adamant that we would never wear a black belt until it was earned. I think that mentality is part of the reason we stuck with it, and finally succeeded.

Either way, it felt sweet to think that we would now be able to walk into the dojo wearing black belts of our own.

8. WILDERNESS YEARS

It wasn't long before we felt that we didn't really deserve our black belts after all. Of course, we showed up at the dojo for training the following Tuesday, proudly wearing our new belts, but Sensei Ray made sure that we were reminded very quickly that we were just beginners. We had to spar with all the other black belts in the dojo. Needless to say, they picked us to pieces. We got the message loud and clear – we were just beginners all over again. There was never any chance of egos getting out of control in that dojo.

My days of winning competitions were also over for a while. As new black belts, we were now the most junior people in the senior black belt events. Although I had fought some black belts in team events before, I was among the most inexperienced competitors in the category. It was tough, but being a black belt is not supposed to be easy.

At my first national championships as a black belt, I was defeated early in the sparring event. I knew the kata event would be tough, but it was worse than I had feared. In the second round I was drawn against Sensei Ray. I knew it was over before it began – he was the undefeated champion for over ten years! I did the best kata I could, but he easily beat me, and went on to win the event ... again. At least I knew there was no shame in my loss.

For the first time, I made our club team for the sparring event. I was the most junior person on the team, so I was put out as the fifth man. It was hoped that we would have done enough to win the round before I went onto the floor, but in a couple of the early rounds I needed at least a draw. Fortunately I succeeded, and we were through to the final, where we were faced by the event hosts, Trinity College Dublin. They had some great fighters, but we felt we had a good chance against them. All the fights were very close, and after four matches it was still a tie. Now it was down to me.

The guy I was fighting was very tall and stocky, probably two or three inches taller than me, and built like a rugby player. I admit that I was quite intimidated by his size. The first minute was very cagey: we were both trying to size the other person up, so we danced around each other as we tried to find a target, with neither one of us wanting to make the first mistake.

After the first minute the referee told us we had to fight or he would give us a warning. Our sparring became a bit more tactical, but we were not fully committed. We remained scoreless. Then, with thirty seconds to go, and with pressure mounting, we both exchanged a series of clumsy, tit-for-tat techniques. As we separated, the referee gave the thirty-second warning. We both thought he said 'Yame', the command to stop, and we stopped fighting. The referee realised this and impatiently shouted at us to keep fighting. I reacted while my opponent was still processing this information, stepped in and launched my favourite technique – jodan mawashi-geri (roundhouse kick to the head). He was still off guard and I caught him perfectly. The referee knew that it should have been a full point, but, even though my score was perfectly legitimate, he may have felt partly responsible because we had thought he had told us to stop fighting, so he only awarded me a half point.

On the restart, I tried keeping out of the way of my opponent, who threw an array of wild techniques as he tried to score. As I danced out of his way, I heard Sensei Ray roar at me. 'FIGHT!' he commanded. 'Win or lose, keep fighting!' I stopped the evasive tactics and held my ground. I tried to time him coming in, but we were back to the stalemate from before. Neither of us got a clean score: time ran out, I had won the fight, and our team were declared the winners. We were the senior men's team kumite national champions.

My first success in a kata competition as a black belt was at a relatively small inter-club competition. I was still Shodan, but Sensei Ray was not competing, and neither were the other most experienced competitors. Even Adrian didn't compete. Before we even started Sensei Ray found me and gave his usual preparation speech. He told me that I should win the event outright. I was surprised, but he gave me confidence, and confidence is crucial in competitions. Before I knew it I was in the final, and my kata, Nijushiho, was enough to win the event.

Later that year I was told that I had not made the national team for the European Championships. I was more than a little disappointed but, to be fair, I had not been a black belt for very long, and had not attended very many squad training sessions. But the reason I was disappointed was because Adrian, my friend and rival, was selected for the men's kata team. Sensei Ray, Martin O'Keeffe and Adrian made up the team that went on to become European champions. Sensei Ray said that Adrian was selected over me because he was the same build as the other two (I was taller and thinner), but in my heart I knew that he was training more than me and he deserved his place on the team.

I had been in University since 1988, so there were times when my training had to take a back seat to focus on studies and exams. It was still more frequent than my parents would have liked, and became a cause of some friction at home. I used to think it was ironic that my mother strongly encouraged me to start karate, and now wanted me to stop, or at least to do it less than I was.

Before I finished college I had been offered my dream job with a major Japanese multinational. I was to go to Japan for two years as a software engineer. I couldn't believe my luck. In the interview process I remember being asked by one of my Japanese interviewers, 'Do you want to live in Japan?' My reply was so emphatic and positive that he just smiled and had no more questions for me, although other candidates that day told me that he had given them a grilling. Unfortunately the job fell through at the last minute so I never got to go and work for that company, and I never got to live in Japan.

After graduation, jobs were few and far between. I took some temporary work where I could get it and eventually, more than six months after graduating, I got a permanent job as a computer programmer for an airline at Dublin Airport. This meant I had to move nearly 200 miles from home. Once I settled into my new life in the capital, and my new job, I started to look for a new dojo to join. I travelled to Bandon every couple of weeks and visited the dojo as often as I could, but I needed somewhere more convenient to train midweek. Such a simple notion became a much bigger problem than I thought it would.

The first issue I encountered was the fact there were no longer any clubs in Dublin affiliated to our organisation. There had been a split a few years previously, and the former chief instructor (who had given me my first double grading) and the guys that I had fought with on the team when I was a brown belt were now all part of a different organisation, and I didn't have contact details for them anyway.

The other problem was that I was used to a particular type and standard of training, and I found it very difficult to find one that was comparable. They say that you don't know what you have until it is gone; I realised quite quickly just how special the dojo in Bandon was. In the first year of my time in Dublin, I must have tried at least six different karate clubs. None of them felt right, and I invariably ended up moving on after a short time.

Surprisingly, the club that I ended up staying at for the longest was not even a Shotokan club. It was a Wado Ryu club that trained in the sports facility beside the airport. When I started with them, I offered to wear a white belt, because I was not a black belt in their style. The instructor thought about it for a minute, then suggested that I should wear a brown belt until I was comfortable with their system, when he would arrange for me to test for black belt. I trained with them as a brown belt for a couple of months, and then one day I forgot my brown belt. The black belt was the only belt in my bag, so I put it on. The instructor looked at me and nodded without saying anything, so I just wore my black belt from then on.

The training was not bad, but it was different from what I was used to in Shotokan. I found the high stances and short back stance particularly difficult to get used to. I still made my pilgrimage to Bandon every few weeks, but it became confusing to train in two different styles at the same time. I came to the conclusion that it was counterproductive, and eventually I stopped going to the Wado Ryu club. For a few years, my training became nomadic. I would train every two or three weeks at a dojo, and practise at home in between. I never stopped, but I became uninspired by the lack of company and the drive you experience from people who push you and encourage you. I felt I had lost my way a little, but didn't know what to do about it.

I was sharing a house in Dublin and I kept a bookcase with my collection of karate books in the sitting room. One of my housemates started looking at the karate books, and expressed an interest in learning karate. When she asked me to recommend a karate club, I found that I could not really endorse any of the clubs that I had trained in, so I didn't know what to do. In the end I asked Sensei Ray for advice. We chatted about my infrequent training patterns, and how I felt a sense of wilderness. I was lost, I couldn't help my friend, and I couldn't help myself. 'Open a dojo,' was his immediate response.

'I can't!' I protested. 'I'm only a Shodan!'

'It doesn't matter,' he told me. 'You have been Shodan for five years now. It will be good for you to have a focus for your training again, and to start teaching others. Open a dojo, and I will help you prepare to test for Nidan next year.'

I had a lot to think about. It was both exciting and daunting. Could I really open a dojo and teach others? Would anyone want to learn from me? Would I have anything to teach them? Could I be called 'Sensei'? Surely I was too young to be taken seriously as an instructor? With plenty of doubts in my mind, but with assurances from Sensei Ray that he would support me, I decided to go for it.

9. SHIN-DO-KAN

I started out small, just teaching two girls at my house. We pushed the furniture in the sitting room out of the way as our warm-up, and then trained as best we could within the limited space. It worked ok, but I knew it was not ideal, so I started looking for a hall that we could rent a couple of evenings per week.

I didn't have a car so it had to be somewhere reasonably close, and it had to be affordable too. After a couple of weeks of searching I found a room in St Kevin's Football Club, in Whitehall on the northside of Dublin. Their main sports hall was not available (or affordable), but they had a smaller room upstairs that was reasonably priced and available. The floor had PVC tiles, which was not ideal, but I decided to take it. The next step was to get some leaflets printed and deliver them around the neighbourhood. I hand-delivered over a thousand leaflets, and hoped for the best.

The first class was scheduled for 10 October 1994. The two girls I had been teaching were both going to be at the dojo on the opening night, but I was worried about whether anyone else would show up. I convinced a friend at work to come along as well, and I asked my younger brother Enda if he would make a trip from Cork for the evening. He had earned his Shodan but had been out of training due to his college commitments. He agreed to take a train to Dublin and come to the class for the first night, as a show of support.

Three new students also showed up that night, so I had a total of seven students on the opening night. It was far from earth-shattering, though it did give me a boost. A new chapter in my karate training had begun. I was now the club instructor of the only SKIF dojo in Dublin, which I had named Whitehall Karate Club. Enda returned to Cork after that first night but student numbers grew over the next few weeks, and soon I had about fifteen students training regularly. In a stroke of luck, my old friend Shane was now also working in Dublin. He came along to help me with the dojo, and we picked up our friendship where we had left off a few years previously in Bandon.

A few weeks after I opened the dojo I received a phone call that was to prove significant to the people at each end of the line. 'Hello Seamus, my name is Garry Cashman. You probably don't remember me, but I used to train in the karate club in Midleton.' Of course I remembered him. Garry was tall and stood out in a crowd. He was funny, popular, and was good friends with Adrian. He would often be heard telling a joke or making a quip in the changing rooms at seminars or competitions: he was always that one person who everyone liked to be around. Garry had also uprooted and moved to Dublin. He experienced a similar struggle around the city as he tried to find a dojo. Like me, he had tried to train independently of a club but missed the camaraderie of a dojo. He had heard that I was opening one, and was keen to have somewhere to train regularly.

I was delighted to invite him to come and join our little dojo, and that was the start of a strong friendship based on a shared passion for karate, which has lasted ever since. It was a good thing for me that Garry came to train with us because shortly afterwards, Shane broke his ankle (playing golf, of all things!) and had to stop karate. I still miss training with him. He was a great karate-*ka*.

Garry and I used to meet up regularly for extra training together, and we worked hard to get our karate standard to where we felt it should be. We took the responsibility of teaching others seriously. I consider the five years Garry and I ran the dojo together to be my second 'golden age' of training. At the time I was encouraged by Sensei Ray, and by the organisation, to take the Nidan (2nd Dan) examination as soon as possible after opening the dojo. Ever the diligent student, I began working on my syllabus with the aim of testing in April 1995. I confess that I took the easy option in selecting a kata for the examination, because I chose to do Nijushiho. In our syllabus, Nijushiho is actually a Sandan (3rd Dan) kata, but I knew it better than any of the ones prescribed for Nidan because I had been doing it in competitions for several years.

I took the Nidan examination under Kanazawa Sensei in April as planned. Some of the senior members of the organisation had formally introduced me to Kanazawa Sensei during the seminar, and explained to him that I had opened an SKIF dojo in Dublin – the first since the split by the previous chief instructor. I partook in my first T'ai Chi classes with him, which gave him an opportunity to get to know me better. With only five of us, the classes were intimate, which afforded us a lot of individual attention.

Kanazawa Sensei seemed to be genuinely pleased that SKIF had a presence in Dublin again, and so he took a personal interest in me. I asked him if he would give me a Japanese name for my dojo and, after thinking about it for a minute, he named it 'Shin-Do-Kan'. He explained that the name meant 'The Club of the Way of Nature', because our karate must be natural.

I was very nervous for the grading, and caught up in the rush of the past few months. Between concentrating on my students at the new dojo and the hurried preparations to grade, I felt quite ill-prepared. I don't think it was the best grading I have ever done. When the results were announced and Kanazawa Sensei told me I had passed, I couldn't help wondering if I had passed because I had opened a dojo in Dublin or because I deserved to pass. There was certainly a nagging doubt, so I committed myself to train even harder, to try to deserve the grade. Garry passed his Nidan examination six months later, and the extra time he had to prepare meant that he did an excellent grading, and deserved his grade without a doubt.

After all the pressure subsided it was time to turn our attention to our students. We held our first gradings for the students shortly after. Sensei Ray came to teach and conduct the examinations. He said he was impressed with all the students, and Garry and I were relieved that we seemed to be on the right track.

More and more people were joining the dojo, and there was a great atmosphere every night at training. Kanazawa Sensei talks frequently about the importance of harmony at many levels. This was something that Garry and I strived for in the dojo, so we outlined some house rules, which we asked students to abide by. We asked for harmony between the students and instructors; everyone should work together to improve each other's standards; no aggression towards anyone in the dojo; and no-one was to look down on anyone else. Everyone was welcome to come and train. Our number one request was to always train with diligence.

10. AIKIDO & BACK TO COLLEGE

I poured all of my efforts into teaching the ever-expanding classes, which soon began to take a toll on my own training. I missed being a student and not having responsibilities! In college I had done a couple of Aikido classes, just for fun, so I found an Aikido club with a good reputation in Dublin and joined it to refocus my training.

The instructor there was an interesting guy. He had been a black belt for twenty years but had never tested beyond Shodan, as he felt it was not necessary. He explained to me that as a black belt he could train in the advanced classes on any seminar, and he could teach, so he didn't see any point in getting higher Dan grades. He had very little ego and an attitude towards the grading system unlike anything I had encountered previously. He didn't facilitate gradings with his students. Everyone wore white belts until he decided that they should be black belts, and that was it. Having come from a culture of different coloured belts with the advantage of measurable and visible progress, but also with the disadvantage of the risk of developing egos, I found this simpler system fascinating.

At first it felt a little strange putting on a white belt, but it was also liberating. Once a week I would take off my black belt, and in doing so, removed the responsibility of teaching and setting an example for my students. I replaced the black belt with a simple white belt for Aikido class. There was no pressure, and no expectation or responsibility when I walked into that class. I was able to just be a beginner and train and learn, and no-one expected me to know things instantly. Most of them didn't even know that I did karate!

I really enjoyed the training, as the emphasis was very different to that in karate. I learned a lot of locks and holds, and throws and rolls. But because of my background in karate, I also learned a lot of more advanced principles, which other beginners would have missed, or not learned as quickly. It was in these classes that I learned about balance, and how to break balance; I learned about the concept of switching (*kaishi*); I learned about absorbing the energy of an attack; and I learned about using an attack against the attacker. These concepts are fundamental in Aikido and are taught to everyone as they begin to learn the art. These skills are often considered 'advanced' in karate classes. Because the emphasis and progression of techniques is different in Aikido, I was afforded the opportunity to learn and practise these concepts more often than I would in any karate class, where they were used as a secondary tool to assist our core training. It was all very interesting, and I brought a lot of it back to our karate classes, especially for the higher grades.

I ended up only staying in Aikido for a few months, which is a pity. Even now, I have promised myself to return at some point. However, an opportunity came up that I couldn't afford to miss. I was offered a position on a certificate course in University College Dublin for Injury Management & Fitness in Sport, from the faculty of Sports Medicine. There were classes on one night per week, plus Saturday mornings, and the evening classes clashed with the Aikido. It was a one-year course and covered a wide variety of modules. From warming up and stretching, to strength training, fitness training, biomechanics and physiology there was a lot of stuff that was directly relevant to our training. These classes were supplemented by modules for first aid, sports massage and the impact of drugs in sport, which were also very interesting.

One of the fascinating aspects of the course was the variety of different experiences that people had, depending on their sporting background. For example, in the module on warming up and stretching, many of the people from ball sports were seriously lacking in this area, whereas the couple of us from a martial arts background were remarkably comfortable with what was being taught because we already followed all the principles involved in our standard warm-ups. Only the person from a gymnastics background had better knowledge on stretching than we did! This diversity lead to some interesting debates both during and after lectures; our banter eventually leading to lasting friendships.

I found myself enjoying my subjects and utilising my newfound skills in the dojo. The coursework never felt laboured and was thoroughly enjoyable. Even exam time was stress free! I was at least as proud to graduate after a year as I had been to graduate from my degree course a few years earlier. And this course benefitted my health, broadened my understanding of the human body, and my students could benefit from the knowledge. It was a win-win.

11. T'AI CHI

I began to study T'ai Chi in earnest after my initial classes with Kanazawa Sensei in 1995. Intimate classes with three or four students took place in a meeting room at his hotel. It was a challenge from the start, but I was willing to learn and study anything that could benefit my karate, so I lapped it up. Kanazawa Sensei explained that he started to study T'ai Chi to help improve his karate, and that this was why he still practised it more than fifty years later. He confided in me that he didn't really like T'ai Chi at first, and that it took him about two years before he started to get a feel for it and actually enjoy it.

As usual, I was different. Although I am sure it took me a lot longer than two years to get a feel for it, I enjoyed it from the first class. Of course I was trying to relate the movements to what I knew; and what I knew was to try to put strength and focus, or *kime*, into every technique. I found it ironic that after listening to Sensei Ray shouting 'Stronger, Seamus!' at me for years, I now had Kanazawa Sensei saying 'Softer!'. Even now my karate is too soft and my T'ai Chi is still too strong! The breathing exercises were simple enough to understand, but learning the movements of the form took about two years. Of course it was difficult because we would only have maybe two classes twice a year at that time, but it still seemed like slow progress.

I was quite surprised when Kanazawa Sensei told me that I was ready to take the first examination in T'ai Chi in 1999, four years after I started studying the art. He explained that there are only six levels in the T'ai Chi ranking system, with the first being equivalent to Shodan (first black belt) in karate. By this stage, Garry and a few of my students had joined me, so now there were maybe seven or eight people in the classes.

The test was as nerve-racking as any karate grading. Although I was only required to perform the Yang-style short form, it felt like it went on forever. In T'ai Chi, the movement must be slow, smooth, balanced and continuous. This is difficult enough at the best of times, but under the pressure of an examination, it seemed impossible. My movement felt jerky and wobbly, and I was quite unhappy about it. Kanazawa Sensei, however, told me afterwards that he understood about the pressure in the examination, and made allowances for the grading. Then he told me that I had passed. I wasn't sure whether to be delighted, relieved or just disappointed in my performance.

I started teaching a little T'ai Chi to my own karate students after that; the regular practice helped me to smooth my movements. After

I passed the second examination with Kanazawa Sensei, I certainly felt that I was progressing. I then began teaching formal T'ai Chi classes to both karate and non-karate students.

There were several incidents during these cosy classes that helped me get to know Kanazawa Sensei as a person, and not just as an awe-inspiring martial artist. I remember realising Kanazawa Sensei actually had a great sense of humour. When he first visited my dojo in Dublin, I gave him a gift of a t-shirt with our club logo on it. A couple of days later we were in Cork for his biannual expedition of karate and T'ai Chi seminars. When Kanazawa Sensei came into the room for T'ai Chi, he had his tracksuit on, and the jacket zipped right up, as though he was cold. As we lined up and he faced us, he dramatically unzipped his tracksuit top and pulled it off to reveal the t-shirt I had given him. 'I'm from Dublin!' he declared with a grin. Over the following years I got to do a lot more T'ai Chi classes with Kanazawa Sensei when I started travelling to his seminars in different countries. The USA, Canada and Scotland, in particular, organised for him to teach T'ai Chi regularly, and I was delighted to tag along in those classes.

Tai-Chi class in Cork, 1995. "I'm from Dublin!"

I took the third T'ai Chi examination in Ireland, but I did the fourth and fifth ones in the USA as they had stopped holding T'ai Chi classes in Ireland by then. It was a real pity: I know a few of my students had shown an interest in studying it, and some had gone on to take their first examination. Only Garry and I kept it up after they stopped the classes in Ireland. In the USA the students were so keen to learn that they organised classes with Kanazawa Sensei on the Friday evening, and then on both Saturday and Sunday morning a group of us would meet in the car park before breakfast and spend an hour or more practising. Kanazawa Sensei's eldest son, Nobuaki Sensei, joined us from time to time. He was a world champion several times over and a fantastic instructor with a natural talent for the art, but in these sessions we all just trained along together. Several of the instructors from the USA, Canada and Scotland also graded in T'ai Chi, and now there is a strong group in each of these countries, teaching Kanazawa Sensei's T'ai Chi to others.

12. TORONTO

In 1995 I began working for an American IT company. The money was better, and I was finally able to afford my first car. This made it a lot easier to get to and from the dojo and I was delighted that I no longer had to wait around for the unpredictable Irish public transport.

At the new company, I had email and access to the internet for the first time. I joined a martial arts chat group called 'The CyberDojo', which included a great group of people with varying levels of experience. Everyone was willing to share their knowledge, and it was very useful to an inexperienced karate-*ka* like me, with only ten years of training. A few months later I was asked to travel to Toronto for a few weeks on a work assignment. I panicked a little at first, worried about how my dojo would run if I was gone for so long, but I spoke to Garry and he assured me that he would be able to look after the classes. It was only then that I started to look forward to the trip. I hadn't travelled very much before then, but I liked the idea of it.

I knew that Sandy, one of the ladies in the Toronto office, practised karate, so I contacted her and asked if I would be able to go training with her. She did Goju Ryu, a very different style to Shotokan, but I was just keen to train and learn. She said she would organise something, so I planned to bring my karate-*gi* with me. Then I had the idea of seeing if anyone on the CyberDojo was based in Toronto, with a view to meeting up and training. To my surprise, a couple of people responded to my query, and we made provisional plans to meet up. I also received contact details of the local SKIF people in Toronto, so between them all I was not going to be short of training while I was there.

Toronto is a beautiful city, but in February it is cold: bitterly cold. While I was there it was regularly minus thirty degrees with the wind chill, and it was common for 30 cm (12 inches) or more of snow to fall overnight. I was worried about how I would cope with training. I was used to training in cold halls with no heating, but not *that* sort of cold! I contacted one of the guys from the CyberDojo, Maurice Richard Libby. We arranged to see each other during the week, when he would take me to a friend's dojo.

Maurice was a revelation. For the first time, I met up with people from another country through karate, and realised that our shared passion for the art enabled us to make friends all over the world. But Maurice also made me realise how lucky I was. When we met up first we talked about our backgrounds. He knew that I was a member of SKIF, but he hadn't realised that I had trained and graded directly with Kanazawa Sensei. By this time I had probably trained on over fifteen different seminars with Kanazawa Sensei, with often four or more classes per seminar. I had taken grading examinations with him seven times already, including both my Dan grades. Maurice stated that he would 'give his right arm' just to train with Kanazawa Sensei once, not to mention actually testing with him. Until then, I had always taken training and testing with Kanazawa Sensei for granted. Over the following years, the more I travelled the more I realised that there were many, many karate students around the world who would love to get to train with Kanazawa Sensei as regularly as I did.

Maurice took me to meet Sensei Michael Walsh at his full-time dojo, which I was relieved to find had heating, as did all the other dojos I visited. In fact, they told me that the temperature was a bigger problem in the summer, when it became too hot and they needed air-conditioning to cool down! I had a wonderful time training with these karate-*ka* throughout my visit. Sensei Walsh was very kind to me from the beginning, which may have been partly because he was originally Irish, even though he grew up in Newcastle, England, and had lived in Toronto for many years. They taught Shotokan karate, but their head instructor also travelled to Okinawa regularly to study other styles of karate and also kobudo (weapon arts). They practised Bo, Tonfa and Sai that I saw, but may have done more as well.

Sensei Walsh was good friends with Maurice, and he invited us both along to a banquet dinner one night. It was a Chinese banquet with twelve difference courses, and I had never experienced anything like it before. It was a celebration for Sensei Walsh and a couple of others, because they were being promoted to instructor status in T'ai Chi. I remember sitting at the meal and enjoying the company of my new friends, intrigued at the notion that two weeks earlier I hadn't even met any of them, and now they were treating me like a lifelong friend. And it was not just Maurice and Michael either – all the others that were there were people that I had trained with in recent days and we had become friends too.

I also trained with the guys from the SKIF dojo in Toronto, which was run by a Portuguese instructor named Antonio Terra. This was a very different set up from the full-time, professional dojo run by Sensei Walsh. The SKIF dojo was run from a hall that they rented a couple of evenings per week, and they didn't have very many students, and no fancy training equipment. But their passion for karate was unmistakable. I loved training with them because they taught the same syllabus that we did in SKIF in Ireland. I started to really understand the benefit of being part of an international organisation. I enjoyed training with them every bit as much as at the other dojo. For the five weeks I was in Toronto, I tried to get to each dojo at least twice per week.

Sandy also organised for me to go to a training session with her Goju Ryu instructor, Sensei Scott Hogarth. When I was going there, I asked Sensei Walsh if I could borrow a white belt, because I felt I should not wear my black belt in a Goju Ryu class. He kindly gave me a gift of a white belt. Sensei Hogarth was an imposing figure but a real gentleman. When I offered to wear the white belt, he wouldn't hear of it, because he had such respect for Kanazawa Sensei. I still have that same white belt, and I keep it in my bag in case I ever visit a dojo of a different style. I even sometimes wear it in my own classes to remind myself – and my students – that the colour of the belt around our waist is a lot less important than we like to think it is.

I thoroughly enjoyed the training, and I even learned one of their basic kata – Gekisai Dai Ichi – which I continue to work on regularly. Although I had trained briefly in Wado Ryu, this was my first time training in a style that was very different to Shotokan, and I was surprised to find that there were more similarities than differences, and that the skills were easily transferable.

Maurice also trained at a Uechi Ryu dojo and he brought me along one night to experience a different karate style. Again, it was a very interesting experience, but I was put with a junior instructor and the low grades because they felt I might not be able to keep up with the class, and therefore my learning was limited that evening. I was still delighted to get to experience even a little from this different style of karate, and all of these small experiences started to add up over time.

One evening at the SKIF dojo, Sensei Terra told me there would be an SKIF tournament that weekend in Toronto, and that Dozono Sensei would be attending. Dozono Sensei was the chief instructor for SKIF in Canada, and I was eager to meet him. I readily agreed to go along to the tournament as a spectator. When I got there, the tournament was already under way. I stood near the entrance, enjoying watching the events in progress. After a few minutes, Sensei Terra spotted me from his position as a judge. He signalled to someone to take over from him, and came straight over to me, with his usual big grin on his face. After we chatted for a couple of minutes, he went to tell Dozono Sensei that I had arrived. He had apparently told Dozono Sensei about me beforehand. As soon as he heard that I was at the tournament he announced a lunch break and came with Sensei Terra to meet me.

Dozono Sensei is a very small man – less than 5 ft (1.5 m) tall. But what he lacks in size, he makes up for in energy and passion. He is like a human dynamo on caffeine. He took me to the canteen in the sports hall and we talked over a light lunch. I liked him immediately. It was obvious that he had tremendous knowledge of karate, and he was close to the Kanazawa family. He asked me many questions about my training and experiences, and my opinion on different aspects of karate. We also talked about T'ai Chi, which Dozono Sensei had been doing for many years. He was pleased to hear that I had started studying T'ai Chi also, and encouraged me to continue my studies. Within thirty minutes of talking, I felt like we were old friends already.

When we went to re-start the tournament after lunch, Dozono Sensei announced that the team kata would be the next event. Then he had a surprise for me as well as for everyone else. He introduced me to the crowd, and announced me as the honorary chief referee for the team kata event! Although I had taken part in many kata events, including team kata events, I had never refereed before. I was shocked, daunted and honoured all at the same time. However, the advantage from the competitors' point of view was that I was independent and unbiased. I was able to judge each performance on merit alone, without any concern for which team was expected to win or any local 'politics'.

In the end, the teams that came first, second and third were the teams that I had scored to place in that order, so overall the other four judges had also agreed with me. I didn't know until afterwards that Dozono Sensei's daughter was part of the team that won. This explained why he was glad to be able to step away from the judging of the event and leave it to someone else.

What pleased me most was that a couple of the competitors from different teams came up to me and told me that they thought I had scored all the teams accurately and fairly. It is always pleasing for the referees and judges to hear that the competitors felt they got it right. Karate competitions, especially kata, can be very subjective to judge, so it is quite common for competitors to feel that the judging was not fair – especially if they didn't win. Subjectivity is always a contentious issue. For example, some judges favour power, some favour technique, and some favour athleticism. Therefore, what one judge considers a good kata, another judge may consider to be poor. This is why most tournaments use a system with up to seven judges giving scores, but the highest and lowest scores are eliminated, and only the middle five scores used. However, it still often leaves competitors feeling that they did not get the scores they deserved.

Unfortunately Dozono Sensei was not teaching in Toronto during my visit, so I did not get to train with him on that occasion, but I vowed to do so at some point in the future. I was sorry to leave Canada, but I knew that I was armed with a lot of experiences and ideas to bring back to my students.

A year later I returned to Toronto for another five weeks. This time I concentrated primarily on the Shotokan dojos of Sensei Walsh and Sensei Terra, because I set myself a specific goal for the trip: I wanted to study something meaningful, particularly in the area of weapons. Although I had done some weapons training with Sensei Walsh the previous year, I didn't do enough of anything to really be able to make use of it when I returned to Ireland. So this time I spoke with Sensei Walsh when I arrived, and I asked him if he would help me to learn one full weapons kata while I was there. He agreed to teach me a Bo kata called 'Shushi No Kon'.

Every evening we did the regular training, and then Sensei Walsh would take me aside and work on the Bo kata with me. Then I went back the apartment and used the handle of a sweeping brush to work on the moves I had learned, trying to get them into my head before the next class. Each night I learned a few more moves, and by the end of the five weeks I had a reasonable working knowledge of the kata.

One night while I was training with Sensei Terra, he told me that I was invited to go to the city of Belleville, a couple of hours away, to train with Dozono Sensei.

It snowed the day I was due to travel to Dozono Sensei, but the Canadians don't let a little thing like several inches of snow deter them from getting around, so neither did I. My car had excellent winter tyres, and all the roads were being cleared and gritted anyway, so driving was not really a problem. I found the dojo, but I was early, so it was locked up and in darkness. I waited about thirty minutes, and then Dozono Sensei arrived, along with his daughter and son. Soon after that, all the other students started to arrive as well.

We had a wonderful training session. Dozono Sensei had been very ill as a baby, and was sent to karate training at the age of four in order to make him strong. Although he always remained small, he certainly had strong spirit and I benefitted greatly from his excellent karate. He also demonstrated his T'ai Chi to me, and explained that he had some karate students who practised T'ai Chi with him, but that he had a lot of students who only did T'ai Chi. He agreed with Kanazawa Sensei's philosophy that studying T'ai Chi was a great benefit to karate. I was very pleased to hear this, and to see his T'ai Chi, because even though I had been studying T'ai Chi with Kanazawa Sensei for about a year and a half, I was still struggling. Talking with Dozono Sensei and watching his graceful T'ai Chi helped make me determined to keep it up.

After training Dozono Sensei invited me back to their house for dinner. He told me that his wife was looking forward to meeting me, so I was delighted to oblige. At home, Dozono Sensei showed me how he had converted one large room into a small dojo for himself. He grinned as he pointed out that he didn't need much space for his dojo, so this room suited him just fine. We had a wonderful dinner together. At the end of the evening, they invited me to stay the night. They had the spare room prepared, which they told me was the room that Kanazawa Sensei always stayed in when he visited. As much as I would have liked to stay, I had to be at work early in the morning, so I had to decline the kind invitation and I headed back to Toronto.

I knew, as my second trip to Toronto came to an end, that I was once again going home with a lot of new knowledge to share with my students. Not only had I succeeded in learning a Bo-Jutsu kata, but I was also full of renewed enthusiasm for karate, T'ai Chi and international friendships.

13. Back Home

One evening as we were starting another batch of beginners' classes, a woman walked into the dojo with a young boy. She had one of my leaflets advertising beginners' classes in her hand. I went to talk to her, and she told me that the young boy's name was Alan and he wanted to do karate. She told me that they had received my leaflet a few months earlier, when I had been advertising for a previous group of beginners. When Alan saw the leaflet he ran to his mother and asked if he could join the karate classes. His mother read the leaflet and saw that I had 'from age seven' on it, and Alan was not old enough. She explained this to him, and his shoulders dropped, obviously disappointed. Several months later, as his birthday approached, his mother asked Alan what he wanted to do for his birthday. Alan produced the leaflet he had kept for months and announced 'I want to do karate!' So here he was, on his seventh birthday, wanting to start karate.

Although I was impressed with the story, as well as his patience and determination to study karate, I knew that some seven-year-olds struggled for concentration and coordination, so I told Alan and his mother that I would take him on a trial basis and see how he got on: but from the first class, Alan was amazing. He paid attention to everything and worked so hard that it was easy to forget he was so young. I could tell immediately that we had someone special in the class. Nearly twenty years later Alan is still training with me, and is one of the key members of my dojo.

After less than three years of training at St Kevin's football club, we were told that they were redeveloping the club, and our room would no longer be available. We had to find a new home, and a search began. What we found was a lovely old building – over a hundred years old – that housed a badminton court. It was part of a large estate that was held by a family trust, on the grounds of Hampstead Private Hospital, which was close to Dublin City University. The building was not in use and was available to rent. I met with the administrator of the trust, and we agreed on a rent for us to have exclusive, full-time use of the building. It needed a bit of cleaning up and some repairs, but it had a lot of character and had a wonderful dojo 'feel' right from the beginning.

I applied to the national organisation for Kanazawa Sensei to come to Dublin on his next trip to Ireland, in order to perform an opening ceremony of our new dojo, and to teach. My proposal was accepted, and we had the honour of hosting Kanazawa Sensei for his first visit to Dublin for over fifteen years. Two senior instructors travelled from Cork to assist with the event, and we collected Kanazawa Sensei at Dublin Airport on the Monday evening. I had booked rooms in a small, family-run hotel for the guests, and I took them all there to get settled in. We didn't have any class that evening, so Kanazawa Sensei was able to have a rest before we took him for dinner. The hotel had given me their largest room for Kanazawa Sensei, and when we brought him and his bags up there, there were three beds in the room. He wondered which bed he should choose, because he thought that he had to share the room with the two instructors from Cork! He was relieved when I told him that they had separate rooms, and that this was all for him.

Kanazawa Sensei demonstrating with me at my dojo in 1997.
This picture was later used on the cover of Shotokan Karate Magazine.

The Chinese restaurant was run by a man named Hong, and I had spoken to him in advance and told him that I was bringing a VIP from Japan to dinner that night. Hong had trained as a chef in Japan as well as in Hong Kong, so he was familiar with both Chinese and Japanese cuisine. When we arrived for dinner that night, he treated us all like VIPs, but for Kanazawa Sensei he was exceptional. He told us that he had gone to the fish market that morning to pick out something special for Kanazawa Sensei, so he would not be ordering from the menu. We all enjoyed a high-quality meal, but Kanazawa Sensei's dinner looked, and apparently tasted, amazing. I don't know what type of fish it was, but Kanazawa was very impressed with both the dish and the presentation, saying that it was done in a Japanese style and was very good.

The following morning we met up for breakfast at the hotel and then Kanazawa Sensei said he would like to go for a walk. We went to the beautiful Botanic Gardens nearby. Kanazawa Sensei loves nature, so he was very happy with this relaxing walk. He stopped every now and then to touch the trunk of some of the larger trees. He would press both hands against the bark and close his eyes for a few seconds, and then he would walk on again. He caught my quizzical look at one point and explained his unusual actions: 'These trees have been alive for many years – mostly older than me. Therefore they have more life experience than me. I am giving respect to the tree, and also hoping to draw energy from it.'

The highlight of the day came after a light lunch: Kanazawa Sensei performed a ribbon-cutting ceremony to formally open the dojo. Although we had been training there for a few months already, this was a very significant occasion for me and for the students. Always the gentleman, Kanazawa Sensei posed for photos with everyone, and then offered to do a few pictures with me separately. He inspected and admired the dojo, before conducting a great class. Even though we had only four black belts training that day, he insisted on giving thirty minutes of training just for the black belts at the end of the class. He went through one of the advanced kata in great detail, with explanations of movements and applications throughout. It was a master class, and we felt privileged to be part of it. It was like private tuition.

After the training Kanazawa Sensei conducted grading examinations for the students, and I was very relieved that everyone successfully passed. We didn't want the occasion ruined by having students fail their examinations that day! When it was all over, we took Kanazawa Sensei for dinner again, and the following morning the instructors from Cork drove him to Cork, where he would be based for the rest of the week.

After he left, Garry and I looked at each other with a mix of relief and elation. We had worked hard to make sure everything would go smoothly, and it had. Although we got to host Kanazawa Sensei in Dublin many more times afterwards, that first time was very special for us all.

Demonstrating with Nobuaki Sensei in Dublin (2009), under the watchful eye of Kanazawa Sensei.

More demonstrations in Dublin in 2009.

14. A Special Year

The remainder of 1997 was equally eventful, beginning with the national championships. It was the first time that I brought my students to compete. At the previous year's nationals I had been beaten by Martin O'Keeffe in the kata event, in the first year since Sensei Ray had retired. I was now determined to try to win the title that Sensei Ray, many years earlier, had predicted I would win and dominate.

I got through to the final with no major issues. There were four of us left, and I figured that one of them was a bit weaker than the rest of us, so it was between three of us for the title. Sensei Ray came over to me.

'This is your title,' he insisted. 'You have to win this today.'

I had been doing Nijushiho in kata finals for nearly ten years by this stage, so this was my kata. After three of us had completed our kata, I knew I was in the lead. But the last competitor had a good kata, and he did Unsu, which is always popular with the judges. He actually *kiai*'d (shouted) three times instead of two, but the judges awarded him high scores anyway.

When the judges counted the scores we had tied for first place. Even using the count-back system, they still could not separate us. They announced that we would have to both perform a kata again to decide the title. Usually the rule in this situation is that a different kata must be performed than the previous one, so I asked if this rule would apply, knowing that my opponent would be at a disadvantage if he could not do Unsu, his best kata, again. After some consultation, the judges ruled that we could repeat the same kata if we wanted.

My opponent did Unsu again, and this time with the correct two *kiai*'s. His scores were high. I knew I would have to pull out all the stops to win and so, for the first time in competition, I performed Unsu. Unsu is an advanced kata, full of technical challenges, and an athletic jump near the end. Most people concentrate on making sure they do a good jump, but often neglect other elements of the kata. My mind-set, as I started the kata, was to focus on each move and make sure that the entire kata felt right all the way through. I didn't focus on the upcoming jump almost until it was done. By not fixating on it, I did not tense up when it came to it, so it flowed naturally and I executed it well. After the final *kiai*, the judges' scores went up, and I had beaten my opponent by two points.

The first thing I did was to seek out Sensei Ray. I reminded him of his prophetic comment in a pub on a Friday night so many years earlier, and told him that this comment had inspired me for more than ten years to try to live up to his expectations. He just grinned and told me that I deserved the title. I held on to that title for the next five years, and then retired undefeated, satisfied that I had fulfilled my obligation.

Our dojo had an incredible day. Twelve of my students had travelled with me to the competition, and for many of them it was their first ever karate competition. We came home with sixteen trophies between us, and then, to top it all off, we were awarded the prestigious 'Best Club Overall' title for the championships. My students were all very excited, and I felt an immense sense of pride in them, but I felt especially good when the instructor from a rival club came over to me and said that he was delighted for me and my students, and that it was good to see a Dublin club back in SKIF and doing so well. His comments struck me as being selfless and sporting, but also very insightful as to what was good for the organisation as a whole and for karate itself.

I was rewarded for my success at the national championships by finally being selected for the SKIF Ireland national team to compete in the SKIF World Championships later that year. They were held in Milan, and I was chosen to compete in the individual kata and team kata.

We failed to make it to the final eight in the team kata event, but with a large number of teams entered, this was not surprising. It was good experience for us, and we came about twelfth overall. In the individual kata, there were a huge number of entries. They decided to split the field in two, and to hold elimination rounds until they got to the last eight of each pool, instead of the usual last eight overall. Each pool had five rounds of eliminations to get through in order to determine the last eight competitors in the pool, meaning that there were around five hundred competitors in that event alone! Unfortunately most of my fellow Irish team members were eliminated after one or two rounds. Even Sensei Ray was unlucky – he came up against one of the Japanese instructors in the third round and was narrowly defeated.

I seemed to have an easier draw, and somehow managed to avoid any of the big names. I was very nervous before the event, and set myself the unambitious goal of not getting beaten in the first round. I had trained too hard to only get to do one kata in the event. After I got through that first round, I relaxed a little. I was pleased to get through the second round as well. After all, only a quarter of the competitors who entered got that far. By now, everyone who was left were of a good standard and I knew it would be difficult, but somehow I got through round three, and then round four. After this, we were told there was one more round to go for a place in the last sixteen. Sensei Ray came and spoke to me to reassure me and make sure I didn't tense up. By now, everyone who was left was of a very high standard. I felt out of place. There were quite a few Japanese left, but also a lot of other experienced international competitors. Sensei Ray knew many of them. It seemed like I was the only rookie. I had seen all the other competitors perform their kata in earlier rounds, and I knew they were all good – much better than me, it seemed. I was sure that my inexperience at this level would show, and I didn't think I had any chance of getting through to the last sixteen.

When my number was called, I stepped onto the floor. I glanced at my opponent out of the corner of my eye. I had watched his kata in previous rounds, and my heart sank. He was good, there was no doubt about that. I didn't fancy my chances against him. The referee called out the kata for us to perform, and I immediately forgot about him; forgot about the judges; and forgot about the crowd. I focused only on my kata. When we finished, the judges raised their flags, and I had won. I was through to the last sixteen of the world championships.

Because of the very high numbers of competitors that started the event, the organisers decided that the last sixteen competitors could do their choice kata, and the judges used score cards to decide the top eight to go through to the final. The standard was very high. My kata was Unsu, but by now the pressure really was getting to me so I did it poorly and did not make it to the last eight. Although I was disappointed to be eliminated at that point, I had achieved far more than I had ever dreamed I would, and got to rub shoulders with some of the best kata performers in the entire SKIF organisation. I had certainly beaten my initial goal of getting through the first round!

Although I did not get to compete in the sparring at the world championships, I had taken part in all the squad training sessions, and my sparring was reasonably sharp. It was a good thing, because a couple of months after we returned from Milan my boss told me that he wanted me to go to Johannesburg in South Africa for a three-month work assignment. I initially didn't want to go, because I didn't feel I could leave the club for so long, but I told my boss, who was a black belt in Wado Ryu, that the famous instructor Stan Schmidt was based in Johannesburg, and if I could get permission to train with him while I was there, then I would go for six weeks. As mentioned before, I had read Stan Schmidt's classic book, *Spirit of the Empty Hand*, when I was a purple belt, and it had been hugely influential on me, so I became quite excited at the prospect of actually getting to meet and train with him. His 'Early Birds' instructor classes in the mornings were famous – or infamous – throughout the karate world, and considered to be some of the best and toughest training around.

It took me a day or so to get contact details for Stan Schmidt. John Cheetham, editor of *Shotokan Karate Magazine*, gave me his phone number, with a slightly tongue-in-cheek suggestion that I conduct an interview with Stan when I got there. I thought that it was actually a very good idea, and I started to think about what I would ask in an interview. I was nervous when I rang the number. Garry was with me, and we couldn't believe we were ringing the legendary Stan Schmidt to ask for permission to train with him. In fact, we were quite giddy as I dialled the number. Unfortunately, I only got his voicemail. I left a brief message explaining who I was, and asking if I could train.

The following day I got a message from his secretary that I would be welcome to train with them. I immediately confirmed to my boss that I would make the trip.

15. South Africa 1997

I arrived in Johannesburg on a Saturday morning after a long overnight flight. I slept a little on the plane, but also managed to read my copy of *Spirit of the Empty Hand* again. I couldn't believe I was on my way to meet the author, and get to train with him. I was met at the airport by one of the office staff, and taken to the apartment complex where the company had booked a number of apartments for the staff on the project. Then I collected my rental car, which was a real bonus, as it meant I had independent transport for getting to training.

I unpacked and did a bit of exploring. The apartment was in a nice area of Johannesburg but it is a dangerous city and the complex had high walls with electric fences on top, with armed security guards at the gates. I decided to have a swim in the small outdoor pool at the complex. Before I went out, I rang Sensei Stan's number and again got his voicemail but left a message, giving the apartment phone number.

The pool was very small – only eight strokes per length – but I had it all to myself. It was a glorious day, with the sun beating down on me, and I was marvelling at how lucky I was to be in such a beautiful part of the world. However, I found that I struggled with the swimming. After just a few lengths, I had to rest, totally out of breath. I tried again, but after just ten minutes I was exhausted. I couldn't understand it, because I considered myself to be reasonably fit. I put it down to being tired after the long flight, and that I didn't swim very often. I decided to call it a day and went back to the apartment to wash up.

Almost as soon as I came out of the shower, the phone rang. When I answered it, the voice on the other end spoke in a deep, booming, voice. 'Hello, this is Stan Schmidt.'

I couldn't believe I was actually talking to Stan Schmidt. He was very friendly, and immediately invited me to training on Monday evening. We chatted for nearly ten minutes, and I was made to feel welcome even just from that talk. As we were finishing up the conversation, he warned me to be careful when I came to training, because I might find it difficult. My first instinct was to think that he underestimated my ability, and that I could take care of myself, but instead of saying this I politely asked him why. 'Because of the altitude, of course!' he said. 'We are nearly 5,000 feet above sea level here. You will not be used to it.' Altitude – of course! That explained why I struggled in the pool earlier. I was used to being at sea level, and the air was a lot thinner here. I certainly was going to have to try to pace myself carefully in the intensive karate classes if I could only manage ten breathless minutes in the pool.

Sensei Stan, as he liked to be called, assured me that he would look after me, and we agreed to meet at the dojo on Monday. He also promised that we would get together and have a chat over coffee at some point, which I hoped might be an opportunity to conduct the interview that John Cheetham had suggested. I resolved to keep a detailed diary of all the classes, which is something that I have done on many of my trips since then.

I was delighted to find that the SA-JKA Honbu Dojo was only five minutes away from the apartment complex, although it was about thirty minutes from the office. When I finished work on Monday evening, I headed straight for the dojo, nervous and excited at the same time. My hands were shaking so much that I could hardly put in my contact lenses when I parked the car outside the dojo. When I walked up the steps to the patio at the front of the building, Sensei Stan was seated comfortably at the top, already wearing his karate-*gi* and chatting with some of the students. As I reached the top of the steps he spotted me, and, guessing immediately who I was, jumped up to greet me, grinning from ear to ear. I bowed deeply and then shook his hand. He introduced me to the other students, and instructed one of them to show me around.

The dojo complex was very impressive. We walked into the reception area first, which was spacious and comfortable, complete with a seating area. Then we went into the changing room. It was smallish, but big enough at a squeeze, and there were several showers. After I changed, we walked back through the reception area, where people were sitting and chatting while waiting for class to start, towards the main dojo. There was a full gym, complete with a fine selection of weights and exercise machines. Beyond that was the warm-up area, which was big enough by itself to hold a class of about fifteen students. In one corner hung a heavy punch bag, and along a wall were three *makiwaras* (striking pads) on wooden posts sunk into the ground. On another wall there were two large mirrors. It was more impressive than most dojos that I had trained in, and this was just the warm-up area.

Then I saw the main dojo. It was large enough to hold a class of forty or fifty students with ease, and was matted wall to wall with interlocking foam mats. The front wall was panelled wood, with the dojo *kun* hanging in a frame. A second wall was covered entirely with mirrors. On the opposite side were glass panels and sliding doors opening out onto a beautifully kept zen garden. It was certainly the most impressive dojo I had ever seen. Just then, Sensei Stan came over to me. Without saying a word, he knew that I was awestruck. He just patted me on the back and said, 'Let's get started'.

Sensei Stan had a relaxed approach to teaching the class, smiling all the time and joking frequently, but the discipline was maintained throughout, and the pace of the class was moderately intense. This was a general class, with coloured belts and black belts training together. By the end of the warm-up I found that my limbs were already beginning to get tired, but I did my best regardless. After the class, I was quite fatigued even though it was no more strenuous than many other classes that I had done. I knew then that Sensei Stan had been wise to advise me to take it easy for a while, until my body acclimatised to the altitude. Over the next couple of days, I spent my time figuring out what my role was at work, and getting to the dojo each evening for training.

On the Wednesday evening Sensei Stan greeted me warmly as I arrived at the dojo. I already felt at home, and I could see why Sensei Stan was so well respected throughout the world. He was much in demand as an international instructor, not only because of his karate knowledge, but also because of his excellent communication skills. Obviously speaking English fluently was a help when teaching in English-speaking countries, but it was more than just that. He had a way of making a point that made it memorable, either with a story or a rhyme, or an explanation that everyone could understand.

After class that evening he called me over to him, and told me he was inviting me to train in the Early Birds with him. I was shocked at this. The Early Birds takes place at the same dojo, but the classes are – as the name suggests – early in the mornings. Membership of the Early Birds is generally reserved for 4th Dans or above, and lower grades were only rarely allowed to train there, and only by invitation of Sensei Stan himself. I reminded him that I was only a 2nd Dan, but he brushed my protests aside, telling me it would be good experience for me.

With Sensei Stan Schmidt in South Africa in 1997.

When my alarm woke me at 5:30 am the following morning I just wanted to roll over and go back to sleep. But I knew I couldn't. I had butterflies in my stomach with nerves and excitement. I had read about the famous Early Birds classes before, but I had never dreamed that I would actually get to train there. I was still half asleep as I put on my karate-*gi* and headed for the dojo.

I arrived at the dojo about ten minutes before 6am. I was impressed to see that the car park was already almost full. I entered and saw that there were between thirty and forty senior black belts already warming up. There were only a couple of 2nd and 3rd Dans, and I was the most junior grade of all. Even in the changing room, the atmosphere was intense and serious, with people contemplating the difficult training ahead of us. I was quite intimidated, and was reminded of my very first karate class where I was too nervous and shy to speak in the changing room.

If I thought it was difficult to cope with the thinner air during the regular classes, this was a different level completely. We started that morning with circuit training as the warm-up, followed by some kumite drills with partners up and down the floor. Next, we split into two groups: under-forties and over-forties. I was to learn that it was never a good sign when we split into groups like that. About three quarters of the class were in the over-forties category, which just showed how long most of these guys had been around. Our group went first, with fast jiyu kumite (sparring) for two minutes. Then we rested while the other group sparred for one minute. That way, we had two minutes of fighting with one minute's rest, and they had one minute's fighting with two minutes of rest. When they stopped, we went again, but with a different partner, and so it went for several rounds.

Suddenly, Sensei Stan stopped the class. Because I was an 'outsider' my fighting style was a little different to their normal style, so he asked me to demonstrate my fighting with my current partner. This meant that everyone was resting while I had to keep fighting, but now it was even more difficult and intense because I was expected to showcase what I did. Sensei Stan stopped us and explained to the group that we should always try to learn from people who come in from different countries, organisations or styles, because they may have small differences that can be good to learn. Then he told all the under-forties to stay on the floor and try to fight 'more like Seamus'. So I had to fight again, although I was gasping for air at this stage.

Eventually Sensei Stan let us rest, and the over-forties went on the floor. I bent over, trying to get my breath, but after a few seconds I noticed out of the corner of my eye that Sensei Stan was coming towards me. I stood upright and tried to control my breathing. 'Please spar with me,' he said in a friendly but commanding voice.

'*Oss*, Sensei!' I replied, with as much enthusiasm as I could muster.

He stood in a high, narrow stance, completely relaxed, and easily shrugged off my attempts to attack. He seemed to barely move, but I couldn't get near him with my fighting that had apparently impressed him so much earlier. Any time I did manage to successfully attack, he immediately hit me back twice with the same technique. 'You touch, I touch,' he said, as he smiled at me. Somehow I felt that my touches and his were not the same thing at all, because his touches seemed to go right through me. I knew he was going to do it, and I still couldn't prevent it.

As we continued to spar I began to rely increasingly on my favourite techniques. Without thinking, my left leg lifted up, feigning an ura-mawashi-geri (reverse roundhouse kick), but then switched to a mawashi-geri (roundhouse kick) at the last minute. This technique had worked for me a lot in competitions. My instep lightly touched Sensei Stan's cheek.

'*Oss!*' He exclaimed. 'Good technique!' For once, he didn't hit me back in the same way – after a double hip replacement a few years earlier, he didn't kick high any more. But he did hit me with a couple of low kicks immediately afterwards, still smiling.

I felt it was more desperation than good, but I wasn't going to argue with him. He was relentless in controlling the fight. Again, I frantically tried to gain some advantage with an ura-mawashi-geri, and then again with the feigned kick followed by mawashi-geri, and I caught him a second time. He complimented me again. And hit me again. Twice. I was getting increasingly tired, but every time I started fading he provided encouragement.

'Restore your energy,' he said at one point, while moving in to choke me with a stranglehold – still grinning at me. 'That is what I want you to learn while you are here.' I tried, but it was not easy. Restoring energy while still going is not the same as conserving energy. One is like trying to go at a steady pace in order to not burn as much fuel, while the other is more like refuelling in mid-air! I vowed to work on the concept over the next few weeks.

Finally he called '*Yame*'. 'You did very well,' he told me as we bowed. I didn't feel that I had done well at all. In fact, I felt like vomiting. He had thrown me around like a rag doll, and before I had even recovered my breath I realised that Sensei Stan had gathered the class around him and was talking to them about me.

'Seamus has done something to me today that no-one has ever been able to do before,' he was saying. There were some sharp intakes of breath from some of the seniors, and people started looking at me. I just looked confused, still trying to regain control of my breathing. What had I done? Succeeded in not throwing up? That had been an achievement in itself. Stayed on my feet? Survived the sparring without having to be carried off? It wouldn't have surprised me if either of those were considered achievements too.

Sensei Stan continued. 'I have never been kicked in the head in my entire life before today, but Seamus did it not once, but twice.' More gasps, and a couple of dirty looks as well. I suspected I might have to watch myself with some of the younger guys.

'I don't know how he did it. It was a clever technique. Maybe we can ask him to teach it to us.' Everyone looked at me expectantly. I wasn't sure what they wanted. I started to demonstrate the technique, but Sensei Stan interrupted. 'No, no,' he said. 'Please take over the class and teach us.'

For the next ten minutes, I – the most junior student in the room – was actually teaching the Early Birds class. That was the type of atmosphere that Sensei Stan encouraged, and was part of what made the Early Birds special. All the students were instructors in their own right, and they were encouraged to contribute when they had something to say. We would often be in the middle of an exercise and one of them would call *Yame*. Then they would explain something or correct something that Sensei Stan had not seen. Everyone would respond with a loud *Oss*, and then we would carry on again. Every training session was tough. Every session had new experiences. No-one went easy on anyone else, and yet everyone was there for everyone else at the same time. It was a fantastic atmosphere and culture of learning combined with incredibly hard training.

After I had been training for about a week in the Early Birds, Sensei Stan told me that Sensei Keith Geyer was returning from a trip away, and would be there the next morning. Sensei Keith was Sensei Stan's son-in-law, and was also the national coach. He said that Sensei Keith was going to invite me to train with the national squad.

The following morning I arrived at the dojo as usual at about 5:50am. It still surprised me how many people were there before me. The place was always buzzing, even that early in the morning. Sensei Stan came over to me as soon as he saw me. 'Sensei Keith is here', he said. 'I want you to meet him.'

He called Sensei Keith, who lumbered slightly as he came over to us. He had a locked knee joint, caused by septicaemia after a motorbike accident some years previously, but he didn't let that or anything else stop him from training. He was a big man, and looked like he punched brick walls for fun. I bowed when he stood in front of me, but he didn't seem very friendly.

Sensei Stan introduced us. 'This is Seamus, the guy from Ireland I was telling you about.' Sensei Keith didn't respond.

'Maybe Seamus could train with the squad sometime,' suggested Sensei Stan. Sensei Keith just said 'Maybe,' and shrugged and walked away. Sensei Stan looked perplexed. For my part, I thought if he had been trying to intimidate me it certainly worked.

After the warm-up, Sensei Stan told us to pair up for kumite. I turned and faced my fellow 'youngster', the only other 2nd Dan in the dojo, but saw a scary sight out of the corner of my eye. Sensei Keith was heading straight towards us. He physically pushed my partner out of the way, and started attacking me just as Sensei Stan said *'Hajime'* (begin). I had never seen anything like this in my life, and I didn't know how to respond. Sensei Keith was a big and powerful man, but his ferocious attitude made him seem even bigger. My youthful tournament-style 'tip-tap' techniques didn't impress him at all, and my efforts just bounced harmlessly off him. He swatted my punches away as though they were no more of a nuisance than a fly. But when he hit me he landed every blow with his sledgehammer fists. I tried to slow him down by increasing the distance and using my favourite technique, mawashi-geri jodan (roundhouse kick to the head). BAM! My shin nearly exploded as he effortlessly swatted the kick away with his massive forearm. Now I could hardly stand on that leg. If it was difficult to face him before that, it was worse now because I was limping. Like an idiot, I somehow thought it would be a good idea to try the same thing with my other leg. SMASH! His forearms were like iron bars. Now both of my shins were throbbing with pain. At least I wasn't limping any more – both legs were equally bad!

We ended up standing toe to toe (because I couldn't dance around any more), elbows tucked in to protect the ribs, and punching each other to the body. Again, my punches just bounced ineffectively off him, while his fists sank repeatedly into my ribs and torso. I could feel every one of his strikes bruising me. Eventually, after what seemed like an eternity, Sensei Stan called *'Yame'* and I got another shock. After being so gruff and tough, Sensei Keith stood back, bowed deeply and grinned from ear to ear at me.

'You can come and train with me and the squad any time,' he said warmly, and shook my hand. It had all been a test – an initiation of sorts. He wasn't willing to be my friend just because Sensei Stan liked me. I had to earn his friendship and respect in the traditional way – on the floor in the dojo. I subsequently trained many times with him and with the national squad, and he is an instructor and a person that I greatly admire.

Just to demonstrate that he had, in fact, been going easy on me during our sparring, Sensei Stan decided later in that class to get some of the 'heavyweights' to demonstrate their punching power. We got a strike shield, and one of the younger guys was told to hold it. Then the seniors – 6th and 7th Dans – took turns to strike it, and the poor guy holding the shield was winded every time, even though they were hitting through four inches of a heavy foam shield. When it came to Sensei Keith's turn, his wind-up was almost like the backswing of a golfer, and then he released a punch that knocked his victim backwards several feet. Sensei Stan grinned at me.

'Have a go holding the pad,' he said. 'I want you to feel Sensei

Keith's power first-hand.' If I thought I had felt his power earlier I was sadly mistaken. I had seen how his punch had knocked the other student backwards, but I figured the student had not been in a proper stance and had not braced properly for the impact. I lowered my centre of gravity, sinking into a deep stance and locking my rear leg firmly into the ground behind me. I stood squarely in front of Sensei Keith holding the pad close to my body. BOOM! The punch seemed to go right through the thick pad and hit me hard in the chest. I was lifted clean off my feet, and landed on my rear end about ten feet away. Everyone was laughing as Sensei Keith strode over and offered his hand to help me up, grinning.

True to his word, Sensei Stan invited me to go for breakfast with him after Early Birds training one morning. While we chatted, I broached the subject of interviewing him. He seemed surprised that anyone would want to interview him, but he agreed to do it.

I had never interviewed anyone before, but I had invested in a little digital voice recorder for the purpose, and I had prepared a lot of questions to ask him. I also made notes of many of the things he said during his classes, and used these as subject material for the interview.

In the end, we actually conducted the interview over several sessions, which was partly down to my inexperience at interviewing, partly due to Sensei Stan's many fascinating stories, and largely due to my desire to meet up with him as often as possible. Although there was a gap of more than thirty years between our ages, and an even larger gap in our relative karate skills, we developed a close friendship during those conversations. I ate at his house on several occasions, and I was even invited out to dinner with him and his family.

Towards the end of my visit, I was in the changing room earlier than usual one morning. There was only one other person in the room, a fatherly 6th Dan by the name of Dave Friend. He started chatting to me as we prepared for class, asking me how I was.

'Sensei, I don't get it,' I confided in him. 'I have been coming here to the Early Birds training for nearly six weeks now, but every morning I still feel sick with worry as I walk in the door. I never know what is coming next, other than another very tough training session.'

Sensei Dave smiled knowingly at me, and put his hand on my shoulder.

'Seamus, my boy,' he smiled, 'I have been coming here for over twenty five years, and I still feel exactly the same way.'

SOUTH AFRICAN JKA KARATE ASSOCIATION

Established 1963

AFFILIATED TO:

Japan Karate Association

日本空手協会 8.11.97

JKA
SHOTOKAN

P.O. BOX 37001 BIRNAM PARK SOUTH AFRICA 2015
TEL/FAX: 27-11-884-9892

Dear KANAZAWA SENSEI,

YOUR STUDENT MR SEAMUS O'DOWD
FROM IRELAND HAS TRAINED WITH ME
FOR THE LAST 6 WEEKS (ON BUSINESS IN
SOUTH AFRICA)

SENSEI, I AM EXTREMELY
IMPRESSED WITH BOTH HIS TECHNIQUE
AND HIS EXCELLENT MANNER. HE
IS A CREDIT TO YOUR ORGANISATION,
AND I EXPECT HIM TO GO FAR
IN HIS KARATE.

I OFTEN THINK ABOUT YOU
SENSEI — HOW YOU MOTIVATED
ME IN THE YOTTSUYA + SUIDOBASHI
DAYS (THE GOLDEN ERA OF KARATE). THANK YOU.
SEAMUS TELLS ME YOU ARE
YOUNG AND STRONG. I WISH YOU
EVERYTHING OF THE VERY BEST! Stan Schmidt

SHIHANKAI: Stan Schmidt - Chief Instructor, SA JKA Karate Association; Head, Africa Region, World JKA; BA., Hons., MA., University of South Africa; 7th Dan, Japan Karate Association. 7th Dan: Ken Wittstock, Johan Roets, 6th Dans: Eddie Dorey, Robert Ferriere, Derrick Geyer, Keith Geyer, Dave Friend, Giel van Tonder, Allen Fourie 5th Dans:, Edward Mtshali. Shihankai Assistants: 5th Dans: Piet le Roux, Ronny Webber., Paul Hlobo, David Nteso.

Letter from Sensei Stan to Kanazawa Sensei in 1997.

In that simple sentence, my fear was put to rest. It didn't disappear, but I realised it didn't have to. I was supposed to feel a certain amount of fear going into those classes. That was part of the lesson, and part of the character development. Feeling the fear and doing it anyway was the challenge, so from that point on I relished it and embraced it. I have taken that simple lesson with me on many other trips around the world. I have visited many countries and trained at the local dojos. I never know what the standard will be like, or what attitude the locals will have to a stranger coming in. There is always an element of nervousness when I walk into a dojo for the first time, but I find that it generally works well to go in with a humble attitude and correct etiquette. Invariably, I leave the dojo with new friends.

My last training session of the trip was a Saturday morning class. Usually the very senior guys (6th and 7th Dans) didn't train in that class, but many of them came along that morning as it was my last chance to train with them all. Before the class, Sensei Stan handed me a letter. It was addressed to Kanazawa Sensei, and he asked me to give it to him when I saw him next. He had written some nice things about me. I was very flattered and slightly embarrassed.

I enjoyed the training session very much, determined to make the most of my last class. Ironically, it was only at the very end that I felt my body had finally acclimatised to the altitude. When the class finished, Sensei Stan made a speech, thanking me for visiting and training with them. The students then gave me a round of applause. I knew that I had made many friends there, and that we would be friends for a long time to come.

16. Back Home – Again

I returned from South Africa on a high. I had never felt so fit, because after getting used to the altitude in Johannesburg, I now had the benefit of it back at sea level. I had learned a lot while I was away, so I spent a lot of time teaching new ideas and skills to the students at Shin-Do-Kan. There was a great atmosphere in the dojo for several months as a result of that trip.

Sensei Stan knew that Kanazawa Sensei was due to visit Dublin soon after I returned home. In addition to the letter he had written for me to give to Kanazawa Sensei, he also asked me to bring two very nice bottles of South African wine as a gift for him.

It is always an honour to host Kanazawa Sensei, and I was delighted that we were getting to do so again. Everyone had been training hard since my return, and we had a lot of students ready for examination.

Kanazawa Sensei arrived after a long-haul flight, and he was obviously very tired. Yet he came straight to the dojo and taught two classes, and then conducted the grading examination. Everyone did well, and he was pleased with the standard. But he was hungry and tired, so we didn't delay at the dojo, and brought him again to the restaurant attached to the hotel. He had liked it there the previous time, because the restaurant manager had looked after us very well.

We enjoyed a wonderful meal and I presented Kanazawa Sensei with the bottles of wine and the letter from Sensei Stan. He read the letter and seemed very pleased with it, promising me that he would write back to Sensei Stan, with whom he had not been in contact for many years. He then insisted that we open the bottles of wine and share them with our meal. Unfortunately for Kanazawa Sensei, he was so tired that he was almost falling asleep at the table, and he eventually decided to go to bed after the main course – it was not like him to skip dessert. Those who remained had to drink most of the wine without him! Even I had a little, although I don't generally drink.

We stayed in the restaurant until they kicked us out, all talking at once about what a great experience it was to get to train with Kanazawa Sensei, and what a privilege it was to get to spend time with him outside the dojo. These meals with Kanazawa Sensei after training became a traditional part of his visits, even though we often finished up quite late at the dojo. Kanazawa Sensei always enjoys spending time with people and having a little fun.

On one occasion I had made a mistake in kata training during class, so Garry was giving me a hard time about it at dinner. Kanazawa Sensei joined in on the joking with a twinkle in his eye. Garry suggested that perhaps I should commit *seppuku* (ritual suicide), and offered to be the *kaishakunin* – the attendant who uses a *katana* to decapitate the person committing *seppaku* after they cut open the belly. Kanazawa Sensei laughed and, with his eyes twinkling, suggested that perhaps there would be a lot of people offering to take on that job! We had many good laughs and jokes like that.

At least, I think they were joking...

17. 1998 EUROPEAN CHAMPIONSHIPS

The 1998 European Championships were held in Sheffield in England. The men's kata team changed slightly, with my old friend and rival, Adrian, joining Sensei Ray and myself on the team. We worked hard together for several months before the event. We met once a week, which meant that I drove approximately 400 miles each weekend for training, and worked on every little detail, right down to breathing together.

Ray and Adrian had been part of the men's kata team that had won a European Championship title some years earlier. They were both a similar size and build. I was quite a bit taller than them, so I had to make a lot of adjustments to my stances in order to keep the overall shape between us throughout the kata, while also trying not to look much taller than them. It is quite a challenge to make stances lower and shorter at the same time. This was definitely the weak part of our team kata. Ideally, I should have gone out in the centre, with the other two either side of me. This would have balanced it out a bit more. But Sensei Ray was our captain, and he had the best kata. Even though it is a team event, the judges often tend to focus on the person in the middle and see the others out of peripheral vision, so it was best that he stayed in the centre. He set the pace and standard for the kata, and we tried to harmonise with him.

The tournament was quite large, with twenty-seven countries participating. I was disappointed to be defeated in the third round of the individual kata, although at least I still avoided my nightmare of defeat in the first round. The team kata event was a very competitive event. There were a lot of teams, and they all seemed pretty good when we saw them practising. However, not many of them were doing Unsu and, because of its technical difficulty, it tends to score higher than other kata – as long as you get it right. Sensei Ray, Adrian and I spent a lot of time together leading up to the event itself. We practised together, and we ate together. We felt like a team, and it showed.

When it came to the event itself our kata felt strong and sharp, but more importantly it felt harmonised. The most important aspect of team kata is for all three people to be exactly synchronised with each other. This demonstrates a high level of awareness and harmony. We were delighted when the scores went up. We were in the lead … but not for long. Another team also did Unsu and scored higher than us, but they were the only ones to beat us. While we were delighted to take second place and receive silver medals for the event, each of us was secretly a little disappointed not to have taken the gold. A silver medal is nice, but the word 'champion' goes with the gold medal. I remember later thinking that silver was just the best of the losers, but I have since come to appreciate that even competing at international level is an achievement, and to win a medal at a major international event should never be a cause for disappointment.

18. Japan at Last

In 1998 I finally got to fulfil my dream of going to Japan. Ever since reading *Spirit of the Empty Hand* and *Moving Zen* in 1987, I had wanted to train there. The previous year I had discussed it with Sensei Stan, and he had strongly encouraged me to go. So when I got married, it was no surprise to anyone that Japan was the honeymoon destination. It was also no surprise that I had a whole month off for the trip.

It was August, and anyone who has spent time in Japan knows that Tokyo gets very hot and humid in August. The trains, crowded at the best of times, become clammy and sweaty. People carry small towels to wipe the sweat from their brows, and the air-conditioning in shops and offices is a welcome relief for those stepping inside.

We stayed at a fancy hotel for the first few days – it was, after all, our honeymoon. When we arrived, I contacted Murakami Sensei at the SKIF Honbu Dojo, and he invited us to go and train the following night. He also recommended a *ryokan* (a traditional Japanese-style hotel) in Gotanda, which was a lot closer to the dojo. It was more affordable, and much more like the romantic notion we had of Japan, complete with sliding screen doors, *tatami* mats on the floors and roll-out futons to sleep on.

We arrived at the dojo at 6:30pm, half an hour before class – there were already quite a few people around – and went into the office to introduce ourselves. Murakami Sensei jumped up to welcome us. Then we were introduced to Suzuki Sensei and Tanaka Sensei and shown around the building.

The dojo itself is on the lower ground floor, or basement, and is small by western standards. It already felt hot and clammy, even with only a few people there. As the class time approached, more and more people arrived, making the dojo seem very crowded. We lined up towards the back of the class, sweating even before Murakami Sensei started the class. When he came out of the office to start the class, he went over to the air-conditioning controls. I was relieved, thinking he was going to cool the place down, but my relief was short-lived. Less than five minutes into the warm-up, the sweat was actually running – not dripping – off the tip of my nose, creating a pool on the floor. It seemed to be getting hotter instead of cooler. At first, I thought it was just that I was not used to the humidity, but Murakami Sensei was grinning mischievously, so I soon realised that he had turned on the heating!

The entire class was a hot and sweaty struggle for everyone, with Murakami Sensei seeming to enjoy it more and more as the students slipped on pools of sweat all over the floor. When the class finished,

67

Murakami Sensei announced that he had put the heating on as a 'special welcome' for the visitors from Ireland on their first visit to Japan. Then he said that there would be a welcome party in the bar nearby straight afterwards.

It was a typical Japanese party. Everyone poured drinks for everyone else, and so we all got to meet and chat with lots of people. Pizza and other food was ordered in, and there was more than enough for everyone. These parties serve an important social function in Japan: they get people mingling and talking to each other, and are a great way to introduce new people to a group. There were some people, Japanese and non-Japanese, who I met that night for the first time and am still friends with to this day, even though some of them are no longer training in karate.

We managed to get on the annual SKIF summer *gasshuku* (training camp), which is not difficult – more of a weekend away with lots of karate. That year it took place in Kawaguchiko, close to Mt Fuji. We travelled by coach, and it was a very friendly atmosphere. When introducing us to people, Kanazawa Sensei made a point of telling people that we were on our honeymoon. On more than one occasion he said something like 'They are training on their honeymoon. They are crazy!'

The training itself was not as tough as I had expected it to be on a *gasshuku*. We had an early morning aerobic session (a run, finished off with piggyback races) for the younger people, with T'ai Chi for the older people. I wished I had been allowed do the T'ai Chi with Kanazawa Sensei, but I was expected to go with the younger group. At least Tanaka Sensei and I won the piggyback race each morning! After the early morning session we had breakfast. Then we had a karate session, followed by lunch, and then another karate session in the afternoon. After this, we were free to do what we liked until the group dinner in the evening.

It was during this weekend that Murakami Sensei started to teach me some Japanese social etiquette. He taught me how to pour drinks correctly, and how to move around the group of people. He explained how to respectfully acknowledge the *Sempai-Kohai* (senior-junior) relationship with each person. He also helped me to understand that although the *Kohai* (junior) does the running around to look after the *Sempai* (senior), the *Sempai* has the far greater responsibility, because they are responsible for the development of the *Kohai*. These lessons have proven very valuable to me down through the years.

We could see Mt Fuji from where we were staying. One day us foreigners were chatting outside. I asked if anyone had climbed Mt Fuji, and a couple said they had. I decided I wanted to do it also. Just then, Kanazawa Sensei walked past, so we asked him if he had ever climbed the mountain. He said that he had climbed it many years ago, when he was young. When asked why he had not climbed it more than that, and he chuckled and said that the Japanese have a saying: 'A wise man climbs Fuji-San once, but a fool does it twice.' It seemed somewhat cryptic at the time, but when I climbed the mountain later that trip, I understood that once was enough.

Back in Tokyo I wanted to visit a martial arts shop to buy a few things. I was told at the Honbu Dojo which station to go to, but once I was there I didn't know which direction to take. I stopped someone walking past, and asked them if they knew where it was, expecting them to point me vaguely in the right direction. Instead of this, the gentleman indicated that I should follow him, and he would bring me to the place. We walked back in the direction he had come from for nearly ten minutes, until he brought me right to the door of the shop. I thanked him and I turned to walk into the shop. I happened to glance over my shoulder and saw him sprinting back down the street – obviously now late for wherever he was going. This is very typical of the Japanese people: they are extremely helpful if you ask them politely for assistance. They feel a sense of obligation to help, and not just in the point-vaguely-in-the-right-direction kind of way. They will help as much as they can. I have had other instances where people have missed their train because they were helping me find the correct platform. This is probably not as big a deal in Tokyo as it might be in some other cities, because in Tokyo there will almost always be another train they can take in a few minutes, but I am still always grateful for their assistance.

The owner greeted me warmly when I walked into the martial arts shop. I bought a few things while he asked me where I was from and with whom I studied. When he realised that I was a black-belt student of Kanazawa Sensei he wanted to know my name, and wrote it out in *katakana* (phonetic alphabet). Then he signalled that I should wait a few minutes and disappeared to an office at the back of the shop. Within five minutes he returned and presented me with a black belt that he had embroidered with my name. I tried to pay him for it, but he insisted that it was a gift. As I left the shop that day, laden down with my various purchases – and my gifted belt – I couldn't help but wonder if there was any other country in the world where the people were so helpful and considerate.

I wanted to travel around and see some of Japan during the trip. Suzuki Sensei made arrangements for me to go and train with his father at his dojo in Utsonomia. His father, also Suzuki Sensei, did not speak any English, but he met us at the train station and took us to his house, which is above the dojo. We communicated with some difficulty through some basic Japanese phrases, basic English and hand signs, while he made us tea and food. As a typical Japanese gentleman, he was an excellent host. When we went down to the dojo for class, things became a little easier. Some of his students spoke English, so they acted as translators when he wanted to have something explained to us. It was fascinating training, and there were several things that he taught in that one evening that have influenced my thinking and training over the years.

After the training we explained that we wanted to stay in a hotel in the area for one night, as we were continuing our travels in the morning. Suzuki Sensei wouldn't hear of it. He spoke to one of his students, and before we knew it our accommodation had been arranged at the home of the student and her husband, and we were all going out to dinner together. In another example of hospitality, Suzuki Sensei refused to allow me to pay for the meal, although I tried to explain that I felt obliged to repay them all for their kindness. In fact, when I tried to pay he put me in a playful, yet painful, thumb-lock, which had me on my knees until I yielded, much to the amusement of the other customers in the restaurant!

I also travelled to Hiroshima, as I had always wanted to visit that city. It was just a one-day visit, but I will never forget it. For a city that suffered incredible devastation and hardship it is a beautiful place, with an overwhelming atmosphere of sadness mixed with determination to overcome, and a simple desire for peace. There are still some types of cancer that are more prevalent in Hiroshima and Nagasaki than anywhere else in the world, due to the after-effects of the radiation. It will take a long time for the radiation to disappear completely, but the important healing – that of a people coming to terms with it and working together for something positive – seems to be well under way. Hiroshima is one of my top ten places in the world.

I had commented to Murakami Sensei early in my trip that I was disappointed to have missed seeing the SKIF All-Japan Championships. When I arrived back in Tokyo after touring around, Murakami Sensei told me that he had arranged for me to watch the JKA Championships instead. He handed me an envelope and told me to bring it with me on the day.

We arrived at the stadium on a very hot day amongst enormous crowds: even the queue waiting to get into the stadium to watch the championships stretched for more than a hundred metres in the blistering heat. Yet no-one complained, pushed or cut in. Everyone was polite and orderly. Uniformed ushers ran up and down the lines, making sure that everyone was looked after and that the process was as efficient and painless as possible.

We took our place at the back of the line and shuffled slowly towards the entrance with everyone else; within minutes many people had arranged themselves behind us, patiently waiting in the snake-like line. One of the ushers spotted the envelope in my hand as he walked past, and asked me to show it to him. He opened it up and read the ticket inside. Immediately he signalled that we should come out of the line and follow him. He led us past everyone and straight into the stadium. I was impressed, but he was not finished with us yet. Instead of directing us to the stairs that gave the spectators a mini workout as they wound their way up to the tiered seating above, he brought us straight out onto the arena floor. He went and fetched chairs for us to sit on, and asked if we wanted some food or drink. Before he left, he made sure that the staff working on the floor knew we were there and were to be looked after, and then he disappeared, presumably back out to the orderly snake working its way in to the upper tiers.

I know why people love to have seats right by the sidelines of a sporting event. It is not so much that you get the best view, although that may be part of it. It is much more about feeling so close to the action that you are almost a part of it. The adrenalin rush you get as a competitor cannot be matched by spectators, but when you are right next to the action it comes pretty close. The only people who were closer to the action than us were the referees and judges. I was itching to get out on the mat and take part. I spent the next couple of hours completely engrossed in the competition.

I had noticed that Tanaka Masahiko Sensei was sitting at the head organisers' table on the other side of the arena. Sensei Stan Schmidt had told me that if I got a chance to meet Tanaka Sensei I should introduce myself and tell him that I was a friend of Sensei Stan. I debated with myself as to whether to go and speak with him, and in the end I decided I was more afraid of telling Sensei Stan that I had the opportunity but passed it up, than I was of interrupting Tanaka Sensei. So I worked my way around the arena and over to the table, bowed deeply and introduced myself to Tanaka Sensei as a student of Kanazawa Sensei and a friend of Sensei Stan. He immediately excused himself from the table and took me for a coffee. We chatted about my visit the previous year to South Africa, and he told me stories about his many visits there. We talked about Ireland, and he talked about his respect for Kanazawa Sensei. Before he returned to his work at the championships, he even invited me to come and train at the JKA Honbu Dojo, but I had to explain that I was leaving in a couple of days, but that maybe on a future visit I would get there.

I had time for just one more visit to the Honbu Dojo before going home. I was glad to be able to thank Murakami Sensei for the VIP treatment I had received from the JKA. He just grinned and told me he had some friends there. I soaked up the atmosphere in the dojo, knowing that it would be my last visit on this trip, but vowing to return again as soon as possible.

I had immersed myself in karate for a month, and squeezed in some sightseeing and Japanese culture, and I had enjoyed every minute. Most importantly, I felt that it had made a big difference in my karate.

19. GASSHUKU

We began to conduct our own annual summer *gasshuku* at my dojo. Sensei Ray and Garry always came along to train and teach with me on these weekends. Garry is an accomplished instructor in his own right. Being a Garda (police officer), his expertise is in self-defence, as well as control and restraint techniques. Everyone always looked forward to his classes, as they were always packed with solid, practical techniques and common sense.

We started on Friday evening with three hours of hard karate training. I used to make the training on the first evening so difficult that everyone, including me, struggled to get out of bed on Saturday morning! Then we started at 7am with a run. The run was split into three groups: one for children, with games such as leap-frog and piggy-backs along the way; one for unfit adults – about one mile; and one for fitter adults – about three miles. After the run we always had a T'ai Chi class, and then a break for breakfast. After breakfast we had our first karate class of the day. Then Garry taught a self-defence class before lunch. After lunch we had another tough karate class and always finished the day with a light session. Sunday morning followed the same format, but in the afternoon we held grading examinations.

The *gasshuku* were always very difficult, and people really struggled with different aspects of it. Some people loved the hard classes but hated the T'ai Chi. Some liked running, while others hated it. I remember one occasion in particular where one of my adult ladies struggled with the run. She was a purple belt, and mother of two small children, but she was somewhat overweight. She was in the 'unfit' group, but really couldn't run at all. She ended up having to walk most of the one-mile course.

She vented her frustration at me initially, saying that I had humiliated her, but really she knew that her fitness was her own responsibility. She apologised to me later, but publicly vowed that she would never let that happen again. She joined a running club, fuelled by the memory of what she saw as humiliation, and fourteen months later she ran Dublin City Marathon in just over four hours. She became extremely fit and lost all the excess weight. She ended up deciding that she preferred running to karate, and continued running marathons. Although the run on our *gasshuku* was a negative experience for her, something very positive came out of it in the end, and I have always been very proud of her achievements.

20. 3RD DAN

After my return from Japan it was time to start to really focus on my 3rd Dan examination. I knew the training the previous year in South Africa, and more recently in Japan, would be of benefit to me now.

I chose a kata that I didn't like very much: Ji'in. I figured that I had chosen an easier kata for my 2nd Dan, so I would work on a kata that I found more difficult this time. I used to go to the dojo an hour before classes were due to start, in order to get my basics and kata training done. Then I would teach two classes, and do some sparring with the senior students to prepare me further. As always, Garry was a big help to me in the months leading up to my grading. We trained hard together, pushing and encouraging each other to be the best that we could be. It was as though my enthusiasm fuelled his and his enthusiasm fuelled mine. Together we generated a great atmosphere in the dojo for everyone else.

I trained in every class, including a couple of T'ai Chi classes, during the seminar with Kanazawa Sensei leading up to the grading examination. On the Saturday afternoon, Kanazawa Sensei decided that he wanted to see some demonstration fights, so Sensei Ray was asked to pick two teams of five to fight each other.

By coincidence, my old friend and rival, Adrian, was beside me on one team. I was all fired up for my examination the next day, but I was anxious that I might get injured in the demonstration fights and not be able to grade. I whispered my concern to Adrian, but he reminded me that we only take one step at a time, and not to worry about the grading until the morning. He was right, of course, so I put the concerns out of my mind and out I went to fight. We had two fights each, and I won both of mine. In the second one, my opponent smacked me on the mouth and split my lip, so I hit him straight back and split his. Sensei Ray, who was refereeing, shouted at us both to have control, but I stole a glance at Kanazawa Sensei, who was smiling and nodding. 'You touch, I touch,' I heard Sensei Stan's voice in my head. Sometimes you have to show that you can take it and also give it. There was no real malice from either of us, and we shook hands afterwards.

When I returned to the line-up after winning my second fight, Adrian turned to me.

'Now who is grading tomorrow?' he whispered, and I knew he had helped me keep my focus that day. The fighting certainly was a good warm-up for the grading.

The next morning I was psyched up for the examination. As I looked around, I could see that there were quite a few testing for 1st

Dan, seven testing for 2nd Dan, and one for 4th Dan. I was the only one testing for 3rd Dan. I wasn't particularly worried about the basics or kata, but 3rd Dan is sometimes called 'fighting grade', and I wanted to make sure that I did well in that section. I didn't know it at the time, but I was pacing up and down the edge of the dojo, eyeing up all the other students. It was only when someone showed me a video recording afterwards that I realised that I had been sizing each of them up to work out how I would beat them.

When I was first called out onto the floor it was for the basics. My legs wobbled a little in the first stance from nerves and adrenalin, but I settled into it and thought I did ok. Again, it was only later that I could see that the kicking combinations Kanazawa Sensei had told me to do relaxed the first time and then with speed and power afterwards were all done at the same pace. It had seemed like speed and power at the time, but nerves have a big impact on performance. The kata section went well. I was pleased that I had selected a kata that was not naturally easy for me.

Then I waited my turn for kumite. All the 1st Dan candidates went out. It took quite a while, because there were about four groups of them. Then the 2nd Dan candidates were called. I expected that they would get one or two fights against each other, and that I would then have to fight each of them, because there was no-one else grading for 3rd Dan. I was closely watching each of them as they fought, preparing myself for my turn.

I expected to be called after the 2nd Dan candidates had finished, but instead the 4th Dan candidate was called out. 'Ok,' I thought, 'maybe I will have to fight him.' I was surprised though, because he was well over forty, and I hadn't expected him to have to fight. As it turned out, he didn't: he was asked to demonstrate *bunkai* (applications) from his kata. He explained the applications first, and then demonstrated them, using me as the attacker. After this, Kanazawa Sensei went through the paperwork, and then announced the examination was finished. I started panicking.

'I got no kumite.' I turned to Sensei Ray, who was standing beside me. I tried to get the attention of the Irish senior grade that was assisting Kanazawa Sensei at the table. 'No kumite,' I mouthed at him, but he just shook his head at me, as if to tell me to say nothing. I didn't want to keep quiet. I was afraid that Kanazawa Sensei would realise afterwards that I had not done my kumite section, and that he would tell me I would have to do it the next time he came over. But more than that, I wanted to do my kumite. I wanted to earn my grade properly. Even as we lined up to bow to signify the end of the examination, I kept repeating 'No kumite' to anyone within earshot. At this stage I must have sounded like a broken record, constantly repeating the same two words.

Kanazawa Sensei said that he would announce the results after the

Kyu grade examinations, and as soon as I got a chance I went over to the senior grade that had been assisting him at the table. 'He forgot my kumite,' I blurted out.

'No he didn't,' was the reply. 'He told me at the table that he saw you fight yesterday, and that this was enough for you to pass. He said that you might be too strong for the other candidates today. You did a good grading.'

What he meant, of course, was that I was too wound up, and my fighting might not have been properly controlled. When I saw the video afterwards, and saw how I was pacing up and down, I realised that he may have been right, but I felt deflated nonetheless. I had trained hard for the grading, and I wanted to pass it properly. Later that day, when he announced that I had passed, I still felt that I had not earned it. In fact, for a long time I felt that I had only received an honorary 3rd Dan, because I did not have to fight. It was quite an anticlimax.

Some years later I reminded Kanazawa Sensei of that examination, and that I felt bad because I did not fight. He laughed and told me that he felt the same way for his 4th Dan examination, because Nakayama Sensei would not let him and Mikami Sensei fight together for their grade. It was just after their famous fight at the All-Japan championships, where they were jointly awarded the title of champion because the final resulted in a draw even after several extensions.

21. FRUSTRATION

It wasn't all good times and fun. Garry got a transfer down to Cork, and so moved back to his home town of Midleton. Having been my right-hand-man for so long, his absence left a void at Shin-Do-Kan. I had been able to rely on him to help out with classes, and I never really appreciated how much pressure he took off me as a young and inexperienced instructor until after he had left.

Most of the other senior grades didn't take much interest in filling the gap when Garry left. While some of them were reliable enough to turn up to class, others seemed to come and go as they pleased. I was left to organise the classes and all the administration that goes with running a dojo. I taught the classes, and it became a big deal if I needed someone to cover for me occasionally. I even had to organise any social events by myself, while everyone else just showed up and had a good time.

I became completely frustrated by it all. It wasn't as though I was making any money from the club. In fact, I was subsidising the running costs out of my own pocket. I was giving the students my time and whatever knowledge I had to the best of my ability. It seemed to be all take, take, take, with nothing coming back from the other side.

One night I returned home after class, having been let down yet again by the seniors. I took my black belt out of my bag and I threw it across the room, announcing that I was quitting. In my frustration and anger I said I was not only giving up the club, but I was quitting karate completely.

The belt stayed on the floor for two days. One of the senior students tried to call me, but I wasn't in the mood to talk. Eventually I spoke to Sensei Ray and to Sensei Stan Schmidt. Between them, they managed to calm me down and gave me good advice. Sensei Stan in particular told me that if I quit, then it would be because my spirit was weak. He said that I could not expect the students to have the same level of dedication as me. It was simply not reasonable. But he also said that if the students were not dedicated, then perhaps their spirit was weak, but if I let that defeat me also then their weak spirit was weakening mine too. He said the only way to beat weak spirit is with strong spirit. Then he asked me how much I got paid to teach.

'Nothing!' I exclaimed, almost offended that he should even ask.

'That's part of your problem,' he said calmly. 'You should be being paid to teach. Your time and knowledge is valuable, but if you don't value it, why should the students?'

I let that sink in for a while. I had always resisted making any money from teaching karate, wanting to be a purist. I could see his point of view though, and I definitely knew he was right about needing to keep my spirit strong, and about expecting too much from the students.

We held a meeting at the dojo, and I explained my issues to the students. We agreed on some changes, and I received better support from everyone. I still didn't take payment from the dojo, but at least I didn't feel that I had to do everything for everyone any more.

22. KANAZAWA SENSEI AT SEVENTY

When Kanazawa Sensei turned seventy I asked him if I could interview him for *Shotokan Karate Magazine*. He stared at me for a few seconds, and it felt like he was looking inside my head. Then he nodded, and told me that someone else had asked to interview him, but he hadn't felt they would do a good job and so he had politely declined. He said that he knew I would do a good job. What was made to sound like a compliment was really a subtle way of telling me that I *better* do a good job!

We did the interview over lunch in a hotel lounge one day after training. I had previously been given the very good advice not to interrupt Kanazawa Sensei while he is talking, because he can come up with amazing stories and wisdom when he is allowed to get into a flow. So I had a list of questions and topics that I wanted to cover, but I used them as conversation starters, and allowed him to talk about whatever he liked, and recorded everything with my little voice-recorder. I only moved on to the next 'pointer' when he stopped talking.

We spent about two hours there, and I only wished it could have been longer, but we had to get ready to go training again. He gave an incredible interview though, the highlight for me being when he stood up and told me to punch him in the stomach. He wanted to demonstrate the difference between internal and external power. So I nervously threw my fist at him, wondering to myself how many people could say they successfully punched Kanazawa Sensei in the stomach. As I expected, my punch bounced off his solid abdominal muscles. This was no big deal – any good karate-*ka* will have solid muscles and be able to take a punch there.

'This is external power,' Kanazawa Sensei explained.

Then he told me to punch him again. This time, my punch sank into his belly. It seemed to almost go through him and all the way back to his spine while he just stood there grinning. He absorbed my strike completely. Then he simply contracted his muscles and repelled my fist back out again. It was a very strange sensation.

'This is internal power,' he stated, sitting back down and talking more about the differences between karate and T'ai Chi, and why he feels it is important to study both. I have been lucky enough to have conducted some good interviews with great instructors, but this interview is the one of which I am proudest.

Later that month Kanazawa Sensei was teaching at a big open seminar in Romford, England, to celebrate his seventieth birthday, so I went over to train. Murakami Sensei was also teaching there with him. There were about two hundred black belts, plus probably another hundred kyu grades training.

The classes were split, with Kanazawa Sensei taking the black belts in the morning, while Murakami Sensei took the kyu grades, and then they switched groups in the afternoon. It seemed that whenever either of them was teaching our group and they wanted someone to assist with a demonstration, they selected me. On one occasion Kanazawa Sensei demonstrated Gankaku-Sho in its entirety, and then had me attack him to demonstrate the *bunkai* of the whole kata. On another occasion, Murakami Sensei was demonstrating some kumite techniques with me, and hit me with an elbow to the back and then swung around with another elbow to the chest. He caught me so solidly that the thud could be heard around the hall, and several people gasped. Even Murakami Sensei glanced at my face to see if I was ok. I wasn't – the strike was still reverberating through my body – but my face didn't show it. I saw a hint of a smile from Murakami Sensei in acknowledgment, and we carried on with the rest of his demonstration.

There was a big party that night in honour of Kanazawa Sensei's birthday. I gave him some Irish whiskey and a crystal decanter, which I was delighted to see some years later in his house in Tokyo. During the party, a large birthday cake was produced. A Scottish instructor was there in his full kilt regalia, and for the cake cutting he ceremoniously handed Kanazawa Sensei his *sgian dubh* (black knife), which is worn on the leg, tucked into the sock. It is an important part of the outfit, and the significance of him handing over this precious item to Kanazawa Sensei was not lost on me. A Scotsman only ever hands over his *sgian dubh* as a sign of true friendship and trust. I was even more impressed when, after Kanazawa Sensei had carefully cleaned the knife when the cake was cut, the Scotsman refused to take it back from the master, instead telling him that it was a gift.

When I got a chance I went over to the Scot, bowed, and told him that I liked his style. When he heard my accent he exclaimed 'You're Irish!' I grinned and nodded, as he followed up with 'Sure the Irish and Scots are all related. We're practically family!' He introduced himself as Jim Palmer, and we became firm friends that night, and have remained so ever since. I promised to come to Scotland to train with them when Kanazawa Sensei next visited, and I attended every visit by Kanazawa Sensei to Scotland after that.

At training the following day, because it was an open seminar with people from different Shotokan organisations, Kanazawa Sensei wanted to demonstrate how different kata are performed by SKIF; and the differences in how he teaches the kata and how other groups perform them. He asked Murakami Sensei and me to perform kata alternately, starting with the basic Heian kata, and working up from there. At one point, Murakami Sensei turned to me and told me that he was lucky that I was there, or he would have had to do all the kata himself! It all went ok until we got to Gojushiho-Dai and Gojushiho-

Sho. Murakami Sensei did Gojushiho-Dai first, so then I was to do Gojushiho-Sho. It is not a kata that I liked at the best of times, but for some reason I lost concentration in the middle of the kata and went into Gojoshiho-Dai. Then I became very nervous and struggled to remember the kata at all. I felt I made a right mess of it, and thought to myself that they would have been better off if Murakami Sensei had done all the kata by himself. I was annoyed with myself, but Kanazawa Sensei brushed my apologies aside with a smile and thanked me for helping demonstrate all the kata.

For me the most important thing was that it was a great seminar and I made a lot of new friends, and that's half the fun.

Helping Kanazawa Sensei demonstrate the bunkai for Gankaku-Sho in Romford, England, in 2001.

23. KANAZAWA NO BO

In 1998 a friend of one of my students came home from Australia to get married. He was a fellow karate-*ka*, so I invited him to come to our dojo to do some training.

When he saw the Bo staffs at the dojo, he asked me if we did much with them. I told him that I had learned a Bo kata in Canada a few years earlier, and that we worked on it sometimes. He told me that he had also learned a Bo kata on a seminar some time previously, so we agreed to show each other the katas. After I performed Shushi-No-Kon, he showed me the kata he knew.

It was a kata I had never seen before, but yet it seemed instantly familiar. I realised quickly that this was because it was much more like Shotokan than the Bo katas that I had seen previously. When I asked him where he learned it, he said he learned it from someone who learned it from someone, who learned it from ... well, you get the idea. He didn't know the full history, but he had heard that it had come at some point from a Japanese instructor who had lived in the UK around the late 1960s. But he didn't even know the name of the kata. I got him to show me the kata a few more times, and by the time we finished I was able to perform it on my own.

I was intrigued. I kept working on the kata, practising it and trying to get a feel for it. In the meantime, I also tried to research its background. I was convinced just from the movements and the feel of the kata that it was created by a Shotokan Sensei.

I tried to find out who the UK instructor was, and when he might have learned the kata. I knew already that Kanazawa Sensei had lived in the UK for a while, and also that he had studied different weapons. I started to read old interviews with him, and found one where he mentioned working with the Bo quite extensively – and came to the conclusion that the kata I had learned may have originated with my own sensei!

I continued to work on the kata, and taught it to my students, but it was some time before I got to ask Kanazawa Sensei about it. The opportunity arose a few years later when I was in Scotland at a seminar with him, hosted by Sensei Jim Palmer. We were having lunch at the home of one of the instructors after training one morning, and a discussion arose about training with weapons. Someone asked Kanazawa Sensei if he had ever trained with weapons and, of course, he said he had done a lot many years ago, but didn't really have the time to do it anymore. At this point I plucked up my courage and asked him if he had ever created a Bo kata. He said that he had, but it was a long time ago. I asked him if I could show him something, and he agreed.

We didn't have a Bo staff, but there was a long hard cardboard tube that I could use. We all went outside – a few Scottish instructors, Kanazawa Sensei, and me with a cardboard tube. I demonstrated the kata, and Kanazawa Sensei's jaw dropped. I had never seen him look stunned before. 'This ... this is my kata!' he exclaimed. 'I have not seen this for twenty-five years! Where did you learn this?' I told him how I had learned it, and that I had deduced that it must have been his kata. He requested I do it a few more times, and made some corrections as we did so. Apparently, I had either remembered it wrong, or someone had made some changes along the way before it got to me.

As we went back to the dojo for the afternoon training session, I asked him what the name of the kata was. He told me that he couldn't remember, so I suggested that we should name it after him. So it was decided, and became 'Kanazawa No Bo'. For the next couple of years, each time I saw Kanazawa Sensei, he would ask me to perform the kata for him again. He would give me one or two corrections and I would work on it again until the next time I saw him.

With Kanazawa Sensei at Edinburgh Castle in 2003,
enjoying a day of sightseeing.

Then Kanazawa Sensei surprised me. He told me that he wanted me to teach the kata to Nobuaki Sensei. He explained that they were both always travelling and did not get to spend time together, so maybe I would get to spend some time teaching his son. This was an honour for me, but it was not such a simple task to complete. I did not get to see Nobuaki Sensei for some time, and when I did there was no time for us to train together with the Bo.

The next time I saw Kanazawa Sensei, he asked me if I had taught the kata to his son. I explained that I hadn't had the chance to do it yet. A few months later it was the same story, so I decided to do something about it. I got a camcorder and recorded the kata slowly and at normal speed from a couple of different angles, and put this onto a DVD, which I gave to Nobuaki Sensei.

A few months later I was in Scotland again with Kanazawa Sensei, hosted once again by Sensei Jim Palmer. We were enjoying a lovely day out on a boat cruise around Loch Lomond, and he asked me again about teaching the Bo kata to Nobuaki Sensei, so I told him what I had done. He was very pleased with this solution. As we talked, he seemed to like the idea of the DVD very much. Then he suggested that maybe I could make a proper DVD of his Bo teachings. I couldn't believe what he was suggesting, but I promised to do whatever I could to help him.

By this time, I was not only doing the first kata that I had initially learned, but I was also now studying the second version of the kata, which had been developed after the first. Because the first kata (now more correctly called 'Kanazawa No Bo Dai') is very dynamic and athletic, the second kata ('Kanazawa No Bo Sho') was developed to suit older or less athletic karate-*ka*. Kanazawa Sensei strongly believes that karate is for everyone, so it made sense that his Bo kata should have a version for both young and old, or for the athletic and not so athletic.

SKIF Headquarters requested that I put a contract in place for the production of the DVD, and provide a draft outline of what would be on the DVD. It took time, but eventually, nearly ten years after I initially learned the kata, I had a formal business contract to do the DVD jointly with Kanazawa Sensei.

24. GEORGE

Shortly after I opened my dojo, a man named George (not his real name) brought his young son to the beginners' class. George used to sit at the back of the class and watch while his son trained. After a few weeks of this, George came to me after class one evening. He told me that he used to do karate himself, but became disillusioned and quit. He said that he had had no interest in returning to training when his son started, but after watching the classes with me, he felt that he would like to start again.

It emerged that George had trained in Shotokan, but with a different organisation. He had attempted for Shodan twice, but one time the grading was cancelled, and the second time he failed. He had quit after this. I told him that he could come and train with us, and there would be no pressure to grade if he didn't want to.

When he started training, I could see straight away why he had not passed his black belt test. His karate was all raw strength, with his shoulders up, and with no real technical ability to speak of. He was strong, but also tense, awkward and rough, with no understanding of correct technique and how to generate power other than with his strength. I set about teaching him our syllabus, and working on refining his karate. Old habits are difficult to change, so even though he tried hard, it took a long time to get him to learn to relax and focus on technique a little more.

Persistence from both of us paid off though, and little over a year after he started with me, George tested for, and passed, his black belt. I was very happy for him, and everyone could see that this was something that he had felt he had to do. He had considered it unfinished business. He felt he had let himself down by quitting so close to his original goal, and there was always a nagging thought of what might have been. It was like a persistent wound, which finally healed when he passed his grade.

George was generally an affable person, and was quite popular in the dojo. His karate was still mostly about raw power and drills up and down the dojo at full speed, but he was learning the syllabus bit by bit. The only problem was that I used to get feedback from students if he ever taught a class in my absence that he would say things like 'Don't worry about getting it right, just go faster and do it lots of times.' I used to smile and accepted that this was part of who he was, and that it was ok: but it was not the philosophy that I wanted people to follow in my dojo, so I tended to limit the number of classes that he taught during that time. His younger son also took up karate when he turned seven, so now father and two sons were regulars in the dojo. This was a nice aspect of our dojo

– quite a few parents and children trained together.

After another couple of years of hard training George was good enough to test for 2nd Dan. When he passed that grading, he gave me a gift of a book, and he wrote in it about how much he appreciated everything that I had done for him. His karate was improving steadily, and he certainly was a good 2nd Dan standard.

The only real issue was that every year in the summer George and his sons would stop training for about six weeks. When they came back in September George would be fine, but the boys were young and didn't have the same retention as their father, so they would have forgotten a lot of stuff. This was frustrating for me as an instructor, and it made it very difficult to get them ready for grading examinations that were often scheduled for mid October.

At the beginning of October one year after George and the boys were only back at training for about four weeks, I was assessing students for the grading examination to be held two weeks later. Quite a few students had not been training as regularly as they should have, and were not ready to grade. I explained this to each of them, and pointed out what aspects of the syllabus they needed to work on for next time. Most of the students accepted what I was saying, but I could see immediately that George was furious that I was not allowing his sons to grade. He stormed out of the dojo with the boys as soon as I finished the class.

I didn't see or hear from him again for a few weeks, and one or two of the other students who were not allowed to grade also stopped coming to the dojo. Then, about six weeks later, he arrived at the dojo in the middle of the class I was teaching and said he wanted to talk to me. When we sat down, his first words were 'I'm going into business for myself.' An interesting way to put it, I thought, as I had never considered the karate dojo to be a 'business'.

'Good for you,' I replied cheerfully. 'I think that will make a big difference to your karate.'

'What do you mean?' He sounded taken aback.

'Well,' I reasoned calmly, 'when you are responsible for other students, and you have to be able to teach the syllabus, it will make you have to learn it in detail. I certainly found that my understanding of the syllabus, and of karate in general, improved a lot when I started teaching.' I shook his hand, and he left. I knew our friendship was over from the day he stormed out of the dojo, but I was sad about how sour it had become over a simple grading.

He opened his dojo a couple of miles away from mine. Some of my students told me that he contacted them directly and invited them to leave me and go to train with him. He apparently promised that students would grade more quickly if they trained with him. One or two students did leave, but most declined his offer.

About a year and a half later, I saw three of my former brown belt students on a training seminar with Nobuaki Sensei. One of them had been refused permission to grade for second brown belt the same time as George's sons were not allowed to grade. When I looked at her kata during training, I could see that it had not improved at all from the day she stopped training with me – yet here she was, testing for black belt. Two other former students were also testing for black belt, and again I could tell they were not ready. I was surprised that they were all being put forward to test.

Unfortunately, all three of them failed. This had a devastating effect on the woman; it shattered her self-confidence and she quit karate completely. I felt very sorry for her, but the responsibility had to lie with her instructor. Too many instructors, in my opinion, want the glory of being a sensei but don't want the responsibility that goes with it. Sensei means teacher, but it has deeper connotations than that. The literal meaning of the word refers to someone more experienced who 'has gone before', i.e. farther down the path, or a guide. A guide doesn't have students; a guide has followers. So although we refer to students of karate, they are followers of their sensei. Therefore, as sensei, we have responsibility for all aspects of our students' development, and we must strive to make sure that their time in karate has a positive impact on their lives rather than a negative one.

To be fair to the other two students who failed that day, they both came back the following year much better prepared and passed their grading then. I was glad for them.

George and his family are no longer involved in karate, and I still think that it is a pity that he didn't recognise that I was acting in the best interests of his children when I wouldn't let them test for a grade for which they were not ready. Had he acted differently, I can't help but think that we would all have been better off in the long run.

25. BUCKET LIST

We often talk about the things that we would love to do but haven't got around to doing yet. There is usually a list of things we would like to achieve before we die, often referred to as a bucket list; that is, things we want to do before we kick the bucket. I decided a long time ago that I was going to try to go and do the things I wanted to do, and achieve what I wanted to achieve, rather than sitting back and just talking about doing them, and later regretting not getting around to them. Specifically, there were certain instructors that I wanted to train with, so when opportunities arose to meet them, I grasped the chances without hesitation.

In 1999 my work took me to San Francisco. I specifically took a detour to Los Angeles for a couple of days on the way home because I wanted to train with Nishiyama Sensei, who was a legend of Shotokan Karate. He had been a senior at the JKA when Kanazawa Sensei was a student there in his early years. Unfortunately for me, Nishiyama Sensei was touring at the time I was there, so I didn't get to see him. I did train at his dojo though, and enjoyed it very much. The people there told me I should come back another time to meet the man himself.

The following year I decided that rather than waiting for another opportunity I would create the opportunity for myself. I had left my job as an IT and project management consultant for a multinational company, and had established a small consultancy business with my wife. My skills were in demand, so I was able to work on client sites and earn enough money to get the business off the ground. Being my own boss, and earning more money, I had a little more freedom than before, so I decided to visit Nishiyama Sensei's dojo again.

I got a special offer on the flights, so I arranged to go to Los Angeles for a few days. I contacted Nishiyama Sensei's dojo in advance and they confirmed to me that he would be there on the dates that I proposed to travel, so I booked the flights and hotel and made the trip.

When I arrived at the dojo for a morning class, some of the students remembered me from the previous year and welcomed me. I was introduced to Nishiyama Sensei. He was shorter than I expected, but he held himself with the proud and determined air of a samurai. At seventy-two, the inevitable effects of age and a lifetime of smoking were starting to show. Although he may have moved slightly slower than the younger students, he had a sparkle in his eyes and a sharp mind that left everyone in no doubt that he was a great karate master.

The class itself was very technical, focusing on detailed concepts of hip vibration to generate power. He discussed different types of *kiai* and had us practise those, and then we worked on kata also. Nishiyama Sensei had an easy-going manner throughout the class, frequently making jokes as he explained what he wanted from the students. After the class Nishiyama Sensei introduced me to Sensei Avi Rokah, one of his most senior students, and suggested that I should also go and train at his dojo in Beverly Hills that evening. He also introduced me to Sensei James Yabe, who had been training in the class with us.

At Sensei Rokah's dojo he spent the class explaining and expanding on Nishiyama Sensei's principles. He was a very good instructor, with an excellent understanding of Nishiyama Sensei's karate and teachings. He taught the same things that Nishiyama Sensei had been doing in the previous class, but he explained them more clearly and in a lot of detail. I got to train in a couple more classes with Nishiyama Sensei and thoroughly enjoyed experiencing some of his ideas and techniques while I was there.

Some years later, after Nishiyama Sensei had passed away, one of the Japanese instructors was looking at my photographs and saw a picture of me with Nishiyama Sensei. He commented, 'Oh, you are lucky. I never got to meet Nishiyama Sensei.'

Pictured with Nishiyama Sensei in 2000.

Another thing that I had always wanted to do was to visit China and observe T'ai Chi in the parks early in the mornings. In 2010 I had the opportunity to go to Shanghai with work. I made contact with an SKIF dojo there before I travelled, so I was invited to go and train with them. That would keep my karate training satisfied on the trip.

My translator accompanied me to the dojo in order to help with introductions. The instructor was a 3rd Dan, and the first question they asked my translator was what grade I was. As a 5th Dan, I was senior to him, so I didn't really want to tell them my grade because this would oblige him to invite me to teach. Therefore, I told her to tell them that I was a black belt, hoping that they would not press for more information, and I would be able to just train alongside them.

Unfortunately, the translator said they insisted on knowing 'what number' in order to know where I should stand in the line, so eventually I had to tell them my grade. Immediately, as I had feared, they asked if I would teach the class for them. Naturally, I was obliged to accept.

They were a great bunch. They trained hard, but they explained that they were lacking in senior instructors in their area. Karate, being a Japanese art, was a minority martial art in China. We had a very enjoyable class, and I was glad that I had a good translator with me, because it made it a lot easier to communicate. Although it is possible to teach a class by demonstrating what we want the students to do and by using the Japanese commands with which all karate students are familiar, it is helpful to be able give corrections or explanations also. While these students were enthusiastic and hard-working, they needed the benefit of some technical details, which I could only give through English.

While it is always great to do karate in different dojos and in different countries, obviously I was more interested in seeing the Chinese arts while I was in China. I asked at the hotel about where I might get to see people practising in the mornings, and they looked at me as if I was asking a stupid question.

It turned out that I was indeed asking a stupid question. 'Everywhere!' was the response. It was true. At 6am in any park people could be seen practising many different varieties of T'ai Chi and kung fu.

I got up early in the mornings and went out to a large park close by the hotel. The first man I watched was probably in his eighties. He practised every morning by himself, moving so slowly but so smoothly. He was incredible. As people walked past they greeted him and he replied, never losing focus or changing his rhythm. I watched him from a respectful distance for a few minutes every morning. After a few days he started to greet me also as though we were old friends.

There were other groups practising sword forms, and several different groups doing various T'ai Chi forms. It was truly fascinating to watch a group of people coming together seemingly randomly, exercising together informally for anything from just a few minutes to maybe half an hour, and then just all going their separate ways again. Even more interesting were the other people in the park –walking their dogs or on their way to work – simply strolling between the people in these groups (I can't call them classes, because no-one was teaching!) as if they weren't there. No-one took any notice of the kung fu, T'ai Chi or sword-fighting that was going on. It was perfectly normal. In Ireland, whenever we dare to train outdoors we have to try to find a secluded area, almost as if we have something to hide, because Joe Public will inevitably start making Bruce Lee sounds or mocking our training in some way. I preferred the Chinese way.

I found a group of about fifteen people who met each morning and practised the same version of the Yang-style form as me. I asked if I could join in and they made me welcome: actually, no-one was in charge so no-one could stop me anyway! It was interesting because they had obviously all learned slight variations from different instructors, so some people did the movements in one way, while others did them in another way. But overall, it was the same form, and I very much enjoyed the experience of doing T'ai Chi with them in the mornings. I was delighted to experience the atmosphere of early morning practice in China for myself.

26. No Bow

Over the years a number of students from other countries trained at my dojo while visiting Dublin. I had several students from Switzerland who came at various stages to study English for a few months, and a lady from Transylvania in Romania, as well as students from other countries. One student who came to me was from a country in North Africa. He was not from SKIF but he told me he was a 2nd Dan, and the national kata champion in his organisation. However, he explained that his religion would not allow him to bow in karate class. I was aware of this issue but had not encountered it first-hand. I wanted to accommodate him, because I have a policy that everyone is welcome in my dojo. At the same time I was obviously concerned about compromising the traditions and etiquette.

I thought quickly, and came up with a compromise. I told him that when we start and finish the class with our formal kneeling bows, he was to stand quietly and respectfully to attention at the back of the class, facing the front. He agreed to this. Then I told him that instead of bowing to his partner when we worked together he could use the western form of greeting and respect: a handshake. Again, he agreed.

It went well for the first couple of weeks. After a little while, the other students in the senior class started to comment that the foreign student was a bit 'showy'. He often took over the whole warm-up area while they waited for the white belt class to finish, so that he could practise the jump in Unsu or some other flashy technique. He also started commenting that we didn't compete in enough tournaments, and that in his country he could enter a tournament every week, and always won.

Although this was a bit annoying we had seen some students like this before, and over time, training in our dojo they learned to tone down their ego and appreciate that there is more to karate than winning tournaments. However, he also soon stopped standing to attention at the beginning and end of class, instead doing some stretches or throwing a few kicks. He also stopped shaking hands when working with a partner, unless it was someone senior to him. I decided to have a talk with him.

Before I got a chance to raise these issues with him, an incident happened in class. I was working on teaching Jitte to the brown belts, so I told the lower-coloured belts to sit down while we went through the kata. Being at the front of the class, I had my back to the students for the first few moves, but when I turned around I noticed that Mr Kata Champion was sitting down also. I stopped and asked him why he was sitting down.

'I don't know this kata,' was his answer.

I was exasperated by his attitude, so I sharply pointed out that the brown belts didn't know it either, and that was why I was teaching it. I asked him how he was ever going to learn it if he didn't join in the class. He didn't answer, and remained seated, so I roared at him to get up and join in. He sullenly stood up and joined in with the class. I was too annoyed with him to speak to him about the other issues that evening, so I let it go for the time being.

About a week later we were in class again, and this time I announced that we would do Gankaku for the black belts. Again, some of the students didn't know it, so I was going through slowly. Once again, I found the same guy sitting down at the back after I had started the kata. 'Why are you sitting down?' I asked him, trying to keep my cool.

'I don't know this kata,' was the predictable response.

I lost it and started shouting at him. I asked him if he hadn't learnt anything from the previous class where we had this problem. I asked him if he knew so much and was so cocky, why it was that he had to sit down when we did different kata? Obviously, I knew it was because these kata were not 'tournament' kata in his eyes, and therefore not important. He had no answers, and just stared defiantly at me. Finally, I just told him to get out, and only to come back if he learned proper karate etiquette. He looked stunned, but left the floor in the middle of the class and never returned.

I had never thrown anyone out before, and have not done so since. I felt bad, but I knew that everyone else in the dojo was glad that I did. He had been the source of negative feeling, and with him gone, harmony was restored. All students, regardless of their nationality or creed, must show the proper etiquette in the dojo.

27. INTERNATIONAL CHAMPIONSHIPS

As I have mentioned before, training in karate enables us to develop strong friendships with people from all over the world. I was lucky that I had travelled a bit to train in other places and made a lot of friends that way, and also forged strong friendships with students who had come to train at my dojo. These friendships really showed their value when we travelled to international events, such as tournaments.

In 2000 the world championships were held in Bali, Indonesia. It was a long way for us to travel from Ireland, so we made a holiday of it. I was delighted to see most of my friends from Switzerland out there, as well as friends from Canada and the lady from Transylvania who had spent a few months training with us. That event really brought home what Kanazawa Sensei has often said about SKIF – the 'F' is for Family.

I got through to the third round of the individual kata in the competition, but was drawn against Tanaka Sensei from the Honbu Dojo in that round, and he defeated me easily. I was happy with the kata that I did, and I figured there was no shame being beaten by someone of that calibre. Although Tanaka Sensei and I had done piggyback races together a couple of years earlier in Japan, I didn't really expect him to remember me. I was quite surprised that when we came off the floor, I turned to bow to him, but he came straight over to me and threw his arms around me like we were old friends.

The following year the European Championships were held in Copenhagen. I felt a lot of pressure for this event. Out of nine senior men competing for Ireland, I was the only one who was selected for all four events: individual kata and kumite, and team kata and kumite.

I felt the pressure, especially for the team kata. Having been on the team that won silver at the previous championships, I was now the team captain, because Sensei Ray had retired and Adrian was no longer training in karate. It was therefore a new team, but we were expected to do well, and we had practised quite hard.

Unfortunately, there was a disagreement between one of the kata team members and the coaches and selectors, with the team member being told the day before the event that he was not selected to compete in the individual events, and that the team kata was therefore his only event. He was very upset by this. By the time our event was due to start at 9am the following morning, he was not in a fit state either mentally or physically to be able to give his best to the team.

I put a formal request to the team manager and coach to replace him with our designated substitute. My request was denied and I was informed that they couldn't drop him because it was his only event. I tried to point out that this should have been sorted before we ever came to Copenhagen, and that he should also have recognised that if this was his only event then he should be focused on doing it to the best of his ability, but it was to no avail. He was on the team and that was final.

Speaking of final, we didn't get to it. In an event with only fifteen teams entered, and where we were fancied to at least get a medal, we came twelfth. I went straight to the coach afterwards and, wrongly, vented my frustration on him. When we returned home I put in a formal complaint about the incident, and it was acknowledged that it could have been handled better. I had had enough though, and announced my retirement from international competitions.

28. SENSEI STAN

In 2001 during one of my phone calls with Sensei Stan, he told me that he was going to be in Scotland later that year. Sensei Keith and a whole team from South Africa were going to be there also, as they were scheduled to compete at the WKC World Championships in Aberdeen. Sensei Stan was to be the guest of honour.

Garry and I immediately made plans to go to over to Aberdeen and meet up with him. Garry was very excited at the prospect of finally meeting such a legend. When I told Sensei Stan that we were going to go and see him, he suggested that he could come to Ireland afterwards and spend some time with us if we wanted. He was looking to take a holiday, and had never been to Ireland. I jumped at the chance and agreed immediately to bring him to Ireland to stay with me.

Out of courtesy, I contacted the JKA chief instructor in Ireland, Sensei Tommy McGrane, to tell him that Sensei Stan Schmidt would be visiting this country on holiday. He immediately asked for a meeting with me, and I met him at a Bewleys cafe in Dublin one morning. As we sat and talked, he wanted to know how I knew Sensei Stan, and why he was coming to Ireland. He explained that he had wanted to bring Sensei Stan to Ireland to teach a seminar for many years, but had never managed to do so. Sensei Tommy wanted to know if we could organise something while Sensei Stan was visiting, and we agreed that it would be an open seminar if it went ahead. Sensei Tommy and I didn't want to make any money from the seminar, so all profits would be given to Sensei Stan.

Of course Sensei Stan loved the idea of teaching a seminar and quickly agreed to the plan. And so, long before he ever even arrived, Sensei Tommy organised a venue on behalf of the JKA group in Ireland, and we invited people to come to a once-in-a-lifetime opportunity to train with this legendary master.

Garry and I were like excited schoolchildren going over to Scotland to spend a weekend with some great karate people. We flew to Edinburgh, hired a car and drove north to Aberdeen. The hotel was a hive of activity. We walked into the reception area, and I immediately spotted Sensei Stan sitting talking to someone I didn't recognise. Sensei Stan jumped up when he saw me, and threw his arms around me like we were long-lost brothers! Then he did the same to Garry. The man Sensei Stan had been talking to stood up and Sensei Stan turned to him.

'I would like you to meet my good friend Seamus, from Ireland, and my other good friend...' he paused and, turning to Garry, asked, 'What's your name again?'

We laughed as Garry told him. It was typical Sensei Stan infectious enthusiasm combined with a little forgetfulness. Garry was delighted to meet Sensei Stan at last, and we found it amusing that he would describe Garry as his 'good friend' when they had never met before. Then Sensei Stan stunned us by introducing the other man as The Prince of Spain! He was Prince Adam Czartoryski Borbon, the cousin of His Majesty Juan Carlos I, King of Spain. Prince Adam was at that time a 5th Dan in Shito Ryu Karate. We bowed, not sure what the protocol was, but he was just there for karate and was happy to join in the conversation.

This was just the first of many surreal moments during that weekend. The following morning Garry and I were treated to a private class with Sensei Stan. Garry had never trained with him before, and had hardly slept that night in anticipation. We were up early because Sensei Stan likes to train before breakfast. He really put us through our paces, and gave an excellent class on Hangetsu. Sensei Stan told me later that he wanted to see what Garry's karate was like, and this was what the class was designed to do. Although Garry was my friend and I vouched for him, Sensei Stan always made his own mind up about people, based on their training in the dojo – a bit like Sensei Keith had done with me a few years earlier.

It was great to see Sensei Keith again as well: we spent a lot of time together, watching the tournament and discussing sport karate versus traditional karate. Garry and Sensei Keith hit it off from the start, much to my delight. At one point they were up in the stands engrossed in a conversation by themselves, so I wandered off to see if I could find Sensei Stan. I spotted him in the cafeteria area, sitting with Sensei Norman Robinson of JKS in South Africa and Ochi Sensei from JKA in Germany. I figured they were busy, so I was about to turn and leave, but Sensei Stan saw me and called me over. He introduced me to the others, and it was Ochi Sensei who invited me to sit and join them. We talked about Kanazawa Sensei and the differences between SKIF and other Shotokan groups, and Ochi Sensei even asked me if I would show them Gankaku-Sho, which I ended up doing in the middle of the seating area. (Fortunately, there were not many other people around, and those that were there were all karate-*ka*.)

We spent about two hours talking. Well, I mostly sat and listened while pinching myself and wondering how I managed to be sitting with these great masters. I even texted Garry to tell him where I was and he texted back to say he was quite happy chatting with Sensei Keith. That was one of the strangest, but most special, afternoons of my karate life.

The weekend went too quickly, but we were equally excited when it was time to leave, because we were bringing Sensei Stan back to Ireland with us.

A funny thing happened when we arrived in Dublin Airport. Garry is a Garda, and Passport Control is manned by members of that force in Ireland. As we got to Passport Control, Garry recognised one of the officers on duty, so we went to his booth. He greeted Garry warmly, stamped Sensei Stan's passport as soon as Garry told him that he was with us, and waved us through. Sensei Stan was visibly impressed, and wanted to know if we knew everybody! Garry replied that he didn't know everybody – only the important people.

We had a lot of fun with Sensei Stan that week. The three of us share the same sense of humour, and there was a lot of joking and laughing, but a lot of respect also. Sensei Stan met my students. He trains every day, so it was natural for him to want to come to the dojo. It was equally natural for me to ask him to teach while he was there, and he was happy to oblige. We had a few private classes as well, including one on knife defences that took place at my office with just four of us!

The JKA open seminar was a great success. Sensei Tommy McGrane was delighted to have a JKA legend in Ireland and to spend some time just talking with him. In my naivety of Irish politics I had sent invitations to many clubs – and this was to get me in trouble later – but I genuinely just wanted as many people as possible to get to train with Sensei Stan while he was in Ireland.

And plenty of people did come and train with him. Everyone who attended loved the seminar, and many people wanted to know if Sensei Stan would return. I had to explain that he didn't travel to Europe very often, and that we were only able to get him to take a vacation in Ireland because he had an obligation in Scotland the week before.

After a few days staying at my home, we took a trip south to Cork. Sensei Stan wanted to travel and see some of Ireland, so we took him to see some of the local sights: we stayed at Garry's house in Midleton for a couple of days and then brought him to Bandon to visit my home town and dojo. Sensei Ray was thrilled to get to meet a man he had admired from afar for many years. He too invited Sensei Stan to teach at his dojo. When Sensei Stan agreed, Sensei Ray let JKA clubs and other clubs in the surrounding area know that there was a rare opportunity to train with the great Stan Schmidt, and again quite a few people were delighted with this opportunity and came to train. Sensei Stan seemed genuinely surprised that so many people knew who he was and wanted to train with him, and he certainly impressed everyone with his knowledge and teaching.

Spending the whole week with Sensei Stan was a fantastic experience, but naturally there were times when it was hard work to try to keep him entertained. Looking after house guests can be stressful at the best of times, even more so when the guest is a VIP. Of course, this was more pressure that we put on ourselves than anything that Sensei Stan did, but there were times when we were happy to have a break if he said he was going to lie down for a rest.

One afternoon in Garry's house he went for such a rest. I had spent some time the previous day teaching him how to juggle, and the juggling balls were still out. Garry and I started trying to juggle six balls between us, which was something I had seen done in Scotland. We became completely giddy at how bad we were at it, while also trying to stifle our laughter in case Sensei Stan woke up! It was the perfect stress relief, so when Sensei Stan finally woke we were re-energised and ready to go training.

All too quickly, the week flew by and we had to bring Sensei Stan back to the airport. Before he left, he invited Garry and I to come to South Africa the following year to stay with him and do some training. We were determined to take him up on the offer.

A few weeks later I found myself having to answer allegations that I was 'bringing foreign instructors to Ireland and running seminars' to the national governing body at a meeting at which Kanazawa Sensei himself was present. I explained my relationship with Sensei Stan and everything that had transpired. I told Kanazawa Sensei that my loyalty was to him and that he would be my sensei always. But I also said that I had an obligation to my students to get the best karate instruction for myself and for them that I could, and it would have been wrong of me not to have jumped at the chance to train with Sensei Stan. Once Kanazawa Sensei heard my explanation and was assured that I had done nothing wrong, he was happy with my responses, so the complaint against me was withdrawn.

A week after this I was in Scotland at Sensei Jim Palmer's house with Kanazawa Sensei, and someone asked him about a particular move in Kanku-Dai. Kanazawa Sensei was explaining why he does the move one way, and also how the JKA does it differently and why. Then he turned to me and asked me with a smile, 'How does Stan Schmidt do this move?' I told him that Sensei Stan does it the same way that he does, because he says it makes more sense. I knew from this brief conversation that he was letting me know that he had no problem with my friendship with Sensei Stan.

29. SOUTH AFRICA 2002

In February 2002 Garry and I travelled to South Africa. Sensei Stan had invited us to stay with him, and this was too good an opportunity to refuse. It meant that we could get up early each morning with Sensei Stan and train with him at his home dojo, unless of course we were going to the SA-JKA Honbu Dojo with him to train in the Early Birds, but it also meant that we spent a lot of time together during the day throughout the two weeks.

Our first morning training in the Early Birds was tough. I had warned Garry about the altitude and lack of oxygen, but when you train in an intense class with intense people there is no holding back or pacing yourself. And the Early Birds was always intense. Sensei Stan started the class that morning with lots of partner-work drills. Then we moved on to sparring. We sparred with different rhythms, starting slow and relaxed, increasing to a medium tempo, and then full speed. Finally, we worked on competition-style sparring. We had several rounds of each type. It was exhausting. Finally Sensei Stan called the class to a halt – but our relief was short-lived. He got all the students to sit down in a large circle; then he called Garry and me out and had us stand on one side, while he picked five guys from the South African kumite team to stand on the other side.

'This is an initiation to welcome us to the Early Birds class,' I thought. I felt slightly annoyed about this, as I had had an initiation of my own when I visited before, but at the same time I didn't really want to leave Garry to have to face it by himself.

Garry went out first. He had to fight each of the South Africans one after another, with no rest. Control was a relative thing, and no-one complained about a little blood in the Early Birds. Garry fought well: he certainly didn't give anyone the impression that he was a pushover. When he finished he was told to wash the blood off his face. One of the other guys went with him to clean his face too.

While Garry was gone, I had to face the same five fighters. It was very difficult because I was short of breath due to the lack of both oxygen and recovery between fights. The locals had the advantage of only having to fight once each – and they were used to the thin air. At one point I was swept to the floor, but as my opponent stepped in to punch me, I kicked upwards and caught him on the cheek. This gave me time to get back on my feet and continue with the fight.

Again, once we had finished a couple of us were sent to clean ourselves up. Despite the cuts and bruises, I should stress that there was no animosity or ill feeling in any of the fights. They were just tough fights, and tough fighters. Karate was taken seriously in the Early Birds.

When I returned from the bathroom, I was just in time to see Garry finish performing a kata, and then Sensei Stan asked him to demonstrate some *bunkai*. It was only then that I realised that this was not an initiation at all – it was a grading examination! But how could it be a grading? I wondered. We were not even part of their organisation. I had no more time to dwell on that question before I was called out and asked to nominate a kata to perform. When I finished the kata, I too was asked to demonstrate some applications and then we all lined up, Garry beside me.

'What was that about?' he whispered out of the corner of his mouth. 'An initiation?'

'No!' I hissed back. 'That was more like a grading.'

In the meantime, Sensei Stan had called all the 6th and 7th Dans into a corner where they were huddled in conversation. I knew then that my hunch was right and that it had been a grading examination. They were deciding whether or not to pass us – and we didn't even know what grade we had just been tested for! And then Sensei Stan walked down the line and spoke quietly to us.

'I know that you are both SKIF students, and you are both 3rd Dan and will be testing later this year for 4th Dan, but I wanted you to feel part of our family in SA-JKA as well. We believe that you are already at 4th Dan level, but it would not be appropriate for us to award you a higher grade than you have at SKIF. Would you like to accept 3rd Dan from us? It will not take anything from your current grades in your own organisation.'

What could we say? We were hardly going to refuse one of the foremost Shotokan instructors in the world. In any case, we knew it was an honour to have been graded by him in this way, and it would have been wrong to appear ungrateful. So we nodded, while Sensei Stan grinned at us. He knew that he had sprung this on us without warning and that we were dumbfounded. He then announced that we had just been tested for JKA 3rd Dan, and that the Shihan-Kai (group of masters) had unanimously approved us to pass. The whole class applauded, and continued to congratulate us enthusiastically in the changing room afterwards.

A few months later I received a package in the post, which contained our two JKA 3rd Dan certificates, signed by both Sugiura Sensei in Japan and Sensei Stan Schmidt. It is the only Dan that I have ever done that was not graded by Kanazawa Sensei. Garry and I used to say we would be excommunicated if Kanazawa Sensei knew about it, but in truth we did nothing wrong; and I view it as an honorary grade from a man that we respect, and who respected us in return. It was only after this 'grading' that I felt I had fully earned my 3rd Dan, because this time I certainly had to show my kumite skills and fighting spirit!

It was amazing to stay at Sensei Stan's house. We got up each morning at 5:30am and had tea or juice with Sensei Stan before going out to his dojo. Although training in the famous Early Birds classes a few mornings each week was a dream come true, we loved our private tuition with Sensei Stan on the other mornings even more. Equally enjoyable was simply sitting around in his house afterwards, talking about karate. Garry and I decided to take full advantage of the situation, and conducted an interview with Sensei Stan – the second one I had done with him, five years after the first. Again, this was later published in *Shotokan Karate Magazine*.

One morning after training, we mentioned that we were planning on going to visit the Lion Park, a small safari park outside Johannesburg dedicated to lions.

'Good idea,' said Sensei Stan. 'I will call Kevin Richardson.' Kevin Richardson is famous throughout South Africa and is known as 'The Lion Man'. He works with all the lions, having raised many of them since birth. The lions accept him as one of the pride. He has featured in many documentaries and news features on lions. What we didn't know is that he had also trained with Sensei Stan, and had even dated one of Sensei Stan's daughters years earlier. Although he no longer practised karate, he was still close friends with Sensei Stan.

Garry, Sensei Stan and me at Sensei Stan's house in 2002.

Kevin himself showed us around the lion park. We saw the lions feeding, and him interacting with them. Of course, we were not allowed inside any enclosures with adult lions, although we could drive around in the main park and see them from inside the car. But he did bring us into one enclosure where there were a couple of young lion cubs. We held and played with a four-month-old cub, which was the size of a large dog. It was as playful as a kitten, and purred like an engine when we stroked it. What an incredible experience.

On our last evening in Johannesburg we trained at the Honbu Dojo as usual. We had made a lot of friends with the students and instructors there, and after class that evening, Sensei Derrick Geyer had a surprise for us. He had organised a party in our honour at the dojo. Everyone had brought food to barbecue and lots to drink. We had *thought* that there were more people than usual at the class!

Sensei Derrick was the official instructor in charge of the Early Birds membership, and at the party he presented Garry and me with our SA-JKA grading books/licences, which stated that we were 3rd Dans and full members of the Early Birds. This was an honour in itself. The flight from Johannesburg to London on the way home was over ten hours, but Garry and I spent the entire time talking about what a great trip it had been.

A few years later, on Sensei Stan's seventieth birthday, we sent him a birthday gift. It was comprised of two parts. The first was a nice piece of Waterford Crystal. The second was wrapped separately with a note attached. The note read: *To Sensei Stan: After your many, many years of dedication to training and teaching karate, providing inspiration to so many people, we feel that you have finally earned this. OSS! Seamus & Garry.* Inside the wrapping was a plain white belt. Sending a gift like this to one of the highest-ranked karate instructors in the world was of course a risk. It was a gift with a double meaning. On the face of it, it was a joke – suggesting that after a lifetime of study he was only worthy of a white belt. But the deeper meaning was the concept of coming full circle – the black belt returning to white, the master becoming the student once more.

Fortunately for us, Sensei Stan both appreciated the joke and understood the deeper meaning. In fact, he even wore the belt to Early Birds training on his birthday. Everyone gasped when they saw him wearing a white belt, and then, with a grin on his face, he read our note. Apparently, some of the younger members of the Early Birds were angry at this point, but the more senior people, like Sensei Stan, immediately saw the humorous side to the gift as well as the deeper meaning, and they laughed.

30. JAPAN 2002

I was sitting with Kanazawa Sensei after T'ai Chi class one morning in April that same year, just a few weeks after returning from South Africa, when I mentioned that I was thinking about going to Japan again soon. He immediately suggested that I should come in August so that I could do my 4th Dan grading there and also to be there for the SKIF All-Japan Championships. I replied that I wasn't sure about grading, but that I would certainly love to go and watch the All-Japan Championships. He said, 'No, no. Not watching. You must compete. Special invitation.'

A chance to be a part of the All-Japan Championships was irresistible. I wrote to the national body and was granted permission to attend both the grading and the tournament. I started to make plans for a three-week trip to Japan.

Nobuaki Sensei kindly invited me to stay at his house for the first week of my visit. We got on well together, so I was really looking forward to that.

I later received an email from Murakami Sensei, informing me that there would be a university *gasshuku* taking place for one week while I was there, and that Kanazawa Sensei had suggested that I should take part in it. A *gasshuku* is hard training, and the university *gasshukus* have a reputation for being the toughest of all. I was worried, but I wasn't being given much choice! I thanked Murakami Sensei and agreed to do it.

I flew from Dublin to London, and got a direct flight from there to Tokyo. When I was sitting on the plane in London, seeing all the Japanese people getting on board, it suddenly hit me that I was really going back to Japan and that I had a tough few weeks ahead. I felt lonely and even a little scared, and wished that I had been able to persuade someone to make the trip with me.

What an amazing trip it turned out to be! Nobuaki Sensei and his wife, Keiko San, took me sightseeing to Naritasan Temple the first day. They made me feel very welcome at their home. Their daughter, Hiyori, was just five years old. She was shy at first, but in no time she was chatting (in Japanese) and playing games with me. I grew very fond of her during that trip. I reminded them that Keiko San had been pregnant with Hiyori when they first visited Ireland.

I went with Nobuaki Sensei to his dojo in Chiba a few times while I stayed with him, and he asked me to teach part of the class. It felt strange teaching karate to Japanese students, but they were mostly children. Nobuaki Sensei kept asking me to teach in English because he wanted to improve his English for teaching in other countries.

After staying at Nobuaki Sensei's house for a few days, it was time to head into Tokyo for training at the Honbu Dojo. I was told that I had to bring my bag, because we were going on the *gasshuku* the following morning. We would be staying at Kanazawa Sensei's house that night, because it was more convenient for getting the bus the next day.

We trained at the Honbu Dojo with Kanazawa Sensei that evening. Most of the other Honbu Dojo instructors were also there. It was a great class, but it was very hot and humid, as Tokyo tends to be at that time of year, so once again we spent half the class trying not to slip on the pools of sweat on the floor. I was delighted that we spent some time working on Gojushiho-Dai in the class, because this was the kata I had been preparing for my grading.

There had been Dan grading examinations a few days earlier, and they presented the diplomas to the successful students at the end of the class. This made me concerned that I had missed the Dan gradings. No-one had said anything to me about when my Dan grading might be on, and it is not considered polite to ask about these things.

After training I was told that we were all going out for a meal to celebrate the successful gradings. At the restaurant Murakami Sensei noticed that I wasn't drinking beer, and asked me why not. I told him that I don't really drink. He asked if there is any drink that I like, and I said that I like a little saké sometimes. He immediately ordered saké for me, and Kanazawa Sensei declared that he and I would drink saké together that night at his house.

Nobuaki Sensei drove Kanazawa Sensei and me back to the house after the meal. His house is amazing. It is quite spacious for a house in Tokyo, although may be considered relatively small in some countries. But it is beautifully decorated, and filled with amazing treasures – gifts he had received from people all over the world. True to his word, Kanazawa Sensei opened a bottle of good saké and poured some for the two of us. I was bemused that Nobuaki Sensei was not offered any, but he was still competing at that time, and was discouraged from drinking too much.

I was very nervous in Kanazawa Sensei's house, worried that I might say or do something that was not correct etiquette; or worse, that I might break something! I was quite relieved when he said he was going to bed, and showed me to the beautiful *tatami*-floored room that Nobuaki Sensei and I were to share that night.

In the morning, we had breakfast together. Kanazawa Sensei prepared a wonderful selection of fresh fruit for us but, after we finished it, he decided that this was not enough so he took us out to a coffee house for another breakfast before Nobuaki Sensei and I headed off.

As we approached the meeting point, I could see the coach that had been hired to take us to Nagano in the mountains for the *gasshuku*. Some of the students were already gathered there. When they saw us approaching, they came running up to Nobuaki Sensei, bowing deeply to him. They took his bag from him, to carry it to the coach. Nobuaki Sensei said something about me in Japanese to the students, and before I knew it they were bowing to me and offering to carry my bag also. In Japan, the relationship between seniors and juniors (*Sempai* and *Kohai*) is very important. Seniors have responsibility for teaching and looking after the well-being of their juniors, and the juniors show appreciation for this by helping their seniors in any way they can – including menial tasks such as carrying their bags. I thanked the students, but carried my own bag. It is not part of my culture to have people carry my bags for me, and anyway I was just a student like them on the *gasshuku*.

The bus journey was over four hours, but the time flew because I was admiring the scenery. Looking out the window I could see the beauty of the Japanese rural landscape, with rivers and tree-covered mountains. I couldn't help but notice that this traditional romantic picture of Japan was starkly contrasted by the modern influence of masses of power lines and pylons cutting through the landscape like scars. As I observed this contrast, I was reminded of Funakoshi Sensei's poem:

To search for the old is to understand the new.

The old, the new,
This is a matter of time.

In all things man must have a clear mind.

The Way:
Who will pass it on straight and well?

While I was pondering all of this, the students were chattering excitedly, looking forward to the week ahead. I suspected it was the first *gasshuku* for many of them, because if they knew what was ahead of them they might not have been quite so enthusiastic. I was aware that we had a week of hell ahead, and was both dreading and relishing it at the same time.

We were staying at a *ryokan* – a traditional hostel-style accommodation. The dojo captain allocated people into shared rooms. Some rooms had two people, but some had as many as six. Traditionally, the instructor (Nobuaki Sensei) should have his own room, but he told the dojo captain that I was to share with him. This seemed to elevate my status among the students, which

I found amusing to say the least. It was nice of Nobuaki Sensei to allow me to share with him, rather than putting me with people I didn't know. We relaxed for the remainder of the day, and Nobuaki Sensei and I went to a local *onsen* (hot spring) to soak and prepare for the hard training ahead.

Dinner was served in the large dining hall. The junior students had to lay out the food for everyone and Nobuaki Sensei and I were called when it was all ready. When we arrived into the hall, the students were standing in front of their designated places. A small table was set at the top for three people: Noubaki Sensei, his designated assistant for the day, and me. Nobuaki Sensei sat down, and indicated that I should sit next. Then the dojo captain sat, followed by each student in turn, according to his or her rank. We followed the same process with the food: Nobuaki Sensei started eating first, then me, and so on. It was very formal etiquette, which was important for setting the tone for the *gasshuku* itself.

As I predicted, the training was very tough. We were woken at six in the morning for a pre-breakfast session. On the first morning we started with a run. I was surprised that it was quite short, but I should have known better. We came back to the car park beside our hostel, where we immediately began sprint-training for thirty minutes, which was exhausting. A few of the students were physically sick and had to continue again regardless.

After the first session we had breakfast, which followed the same formal routine as the night before. Then it was time to get ready for the real training: two hours of hard karate before lunch. After lunch, it was another two hours of hard karate. No-one was allowed to stop or even slow down. We regularly faced one another during basics, so we couldn't miss a single count or we would look bad in front of our partner. There were lots of repetitions of techniques at high speed. People pushed and encouraged each other constantly. It was very hot and humid, so we had some breaks in between exercises for drinks. For every break, one of the white belts would bring a drink to Nobuaki Sensei and me.

I understood the *Sempai-Kohai* relationship, and how the juniors look after their seniors out of respect. I also understood that the seniors did a lot more for the juniors, by looking after their overall welfare and teaching them. Therefore, I felt very bad that I was being treated as a senior, because I was an outsider, and didn't feel I had earned that right. I felt I was not actually doing anything to help the junior students. But they didn't seem to mind. On one occasion while we walked to the dojo, one of the white belts came up to me and offered to carry my small towel – the only thing I had in my hand. His English was better than that of most of the other students, so we talked a little as we walked together. He told me that they were grateful and honoured that I went there to train with them, and that the students admired my karate. Maybe I did give something back after all, without even realising it.

Each day the training changed. For some of the morning sessions we just ran up the mountain, and for others we did all kata. Most of the karate classes had a lot of basics, but each class had something different. What they all had in common was that they were tough. Very tough.

Training barefoot can be hard on the feet, and blisters are common for the first few years until the feet toughen up. On a *gasshuku* like this, most of the students developed blisters. In some cases the skin had come off, to reveal raw skin underneath, and then the raw skin developed blisters too. Some of the students had to cover their feet with tape. Most students also had bruises the length of their forearms and all down their shins, but no-one complained and no-one stopped training.

My feet were ok as they hadn't blistered in years, but after a couple of days I started to feel very weak and queasy. It was not from the training; I had contracted a stomach bug. I simply couldn't face eating, and sometimes stayed in the room and slept at meal times. I was vomiting, and it was obvious to everyone that I was ill. What terrible timing. Nobuaki Sensei could see that I was unwell before I even said anything. He told me that I should not train on the third day. He said I should rest and try to be better for the next day because Murakami Sensei would be replacing him as the instructor for the second half of the week, and I 'would need all my strength'.

I was tempted to take a day off, but I knew that I couldn't. If the college kids could train with blistered feet, I could train with a weak stomach. I pulled on my karate-*gi*, and stubbornly went out with the rest of them. I vomited during the sprints, but kept going and completed about thirty minutes of the forty-five minute session. I had to sit down for the last few minutes, but as several others were also sitting down, I was not alone. The rest of that day was difficult. My techniques were weak and slow, but all the other students encouraged me to keep going. That is the Japanese way.

Murakami Sensei arrived that afternoon to replace Nobuaki Sensei, and although he was surprised that I was in the Sensei's room, he allowed me to stay with him. We had a lot of fun over the next few days, although I was still quite ill for the remainder of the *gasshuku*.

I asked Murakami Sensei if he would take a look at my kata for me, although I didn't actually mention the possibility of grading. He got me to perform it before the afternoon session on one of the days, with all the students watching. After I finished, he considered it for a minute. 'You are like a singer with a good voice,' he started, 'but who is only singing one note. Your kata is all the same rhythm and tone. Please try to express the rhythm of the kata more correctly.' I struggled to comprehend how I should do that, but it gave me something new to think about over the next few days. Actually, it was only after I returned home from Japan that I suddenly understood what he had wanted. I immediately wanted to get on a plane and go back to Japan again to show Murakami Sensei. It just shows that the benefits of intensive training often come long after the training itself.

On the second-last day of the *gasshuku*, one of the brown belts who had just passed his Shodan during the week came and asked me if I would help him work on *Empi* (a black belt kata) after dinner. I asked Murakami Sensei if this was ok, and he said it was, so I spent some time helping correct the student's kata. A few others watched as well. I was glad to be able to give them back something tangible for all their help and kindness to me.

Later that evening, Murakami Sensei and I went to the *onsen* together, and I asked him why the training was so tough. I pointed out that the students all had skinned feet and bruises all over. They really were suffering. Murakami Sensei explained that a lot of the university students would only ever train in karate while at university. After they graduate, many of them become career 'salary men', and don't have time for karate. Therefore, teaching them technique would be of very little benefit to them in the long term. But with hard training, they learn to have strong spirit, and this is something that will stay with them throughout their lives.

Having taught some self-defence classes in the past, I had very quickly realised the futility of teaching people techniques that they would forget long before they ever needed to use them, so I felt there was a lot of wisdom in this approach to teaching 'short-term' students. At least they were learning about their abilities to achieve far more than they would have thought possible, and that this would give them an indomitable spirit, which would be valuable to them in many aspects of their lives.

The last day of the *gasshuku* was the toughest of all. By now, almost all of the students had their feet taped up to protect the raw skin, and each arm seemed to have just one large bruise from elbow to wrist. The pre-breakfast session set the tone for the day. We had a thirty-minute run first. Then we lined up in the car park outside our hostel for the real training. First we did several kata a few times each. After this, Murakami Sensei made all thirty of us form a circle, and stand in kiba-dachi. From there, we each had to count out ten punches, so one time around the circle was three hundred punches, all while Murakami Sensei was going around giving a kick to anyone who was not in a deep enough stance. Our legs were burning from the strain. When we got around the circle we thought we were done, but we were wrong: Murakami

Sensei told us to keep going, a second time around the circle. Six hundred punches. And then we went around a third time. Nine hundred punches. And then ten more people to count out the last hundred to make it a thousand punches in total. We were nearly twenty minutes holding that stance and punching. Most people collapsed onto the tarmac when we were eventually allowed to stop. Certainly my legs wobbled all the way back to my room, as Murakami Sensei cheerfully told me that he wanted to 'make a memory' for the students. I think he succeeded – I certainly have never forgotten it!

The rest of the day was a blur of brutally tough training, but finally it was over and we had completed the *gasshuku*. I was reminded of someone who had commented about a *gasshuku* before by saying '*gasshuku* is very hard training – only happy when it is over.' We certainly all felt elated now that it was finished.

When we went back to Tokyo the next day, I had hoped to get to the Honbu Dojo, but Nobuaki Sensei came to bring me back to Chiba immediately. I was surprised to find myself disappointed not to be going training. After all, it was just one day after the toughest week of training of my life. It probably helped that my bug seemed to have passed, and I was feeling a bit better. I even had my appetite back. I was glad when Nobuaki Sensei and his wife took me out for dinner that evening.

A couple of days later, Nobuaki Sensei and I were on the train from Chiba to Tokyo together, and he casually mentioned that my grading examination would be after class that morning. I got a bit of a shock, because I had almost forgotten about it. I had been distracted on the *gasshuku*, and no-one had said anything about the grading. In a way, this was better because I didn't really have time to worry about it.

Kanazawa Sensei taught the class that morning. There were a lot of instructors from other dojos there, and we spent the class going through the syllabus, concentrating especially and in great detail on the kumite syllabus to make sure that everyone was doing it the same way. All the Honbu Dojo instructors were training in the class also.

When the class finished, Kanazawa Sensei announced that the grading examination would start in five minutes, and he left to change into his formal clothes. Murakami Sensei, Nobuaki Sensei and Tanaka Sensei stayed on the floor and started warming up and practising sparring techniques, as though they were preparing for fighting. I wondered if they were also testing. My heart sank. I knew I would have to fight for 4th Dan, but I didn't think I was going to have to fight those guys. I was thinking that it was ironic that I complained about not having to do any fighting for my 3rd Dan, and now was complaining to myself that I was going to have to fight the instructors. Fortunately, I shrugged off the concerns and reminded myself of the fighting I had done in South Africa earlier that year. I steeled my nerves and told myself that I wasn't going to be expected to beat them. I would only have to keep getting up each time they knocked me over. I was as ready as I ever would be.

When Kanazawa Sensei returned and announced the start of the grading and told us to line up, the three instructors disappeared into the changing room. I wasn't going to have to fight them after all! It had just been a psychological ploy to try to frighten those of us who were grading.

After that scare, the actual grading was manageable. I had a couple of tough fights, but I felt I did well enough. I was worried about the kata, especially after Murakami Sensei's comments during the *gasshuku*. It was a relief when I was told that I had passed. It was a dream come true to grade in Japan, but it was especially important for me to see that I could come to a different country and still hold my own. Whether it was true or not, I felt that I had to earn my grade all the more in the Honbu Dojo in Japan than I would at home.

The All-Japan Championships were on that weekend. As part of the Honbu Dojo demonstration at the championships, Kanazawa Sensei had asked me and a Belgian student named Eric to do a demonstration of Jiyu-Ippon Kumite (semi-freestyle) together, with a pair of Japanese students doing a simultaneous demonstration. It was an honour to be asked to take part in this demonstration, so Eric and I practised together several times in the days leading up to the championships.

At the championships, all the teams paraded out into the arena, with the club banner held up in front. I was very proud to walk out under the banner of the Honbu Dojo. I had never been beaten in the first round of any kata competition, but when I looked around me I realised I was the only foreigner taking part in this event, and that all the judges were Japanese too. I imagined that all the competitors must be fantastic – and some of them were. In addition to several of the Honbu Dojo instructors, I recognised others from international competitions as well. I figured that I might have to accept defeat in the first round, in exchange for the honour of being there.

I was wrong. I somehow managed to get through three rounds of kata. At that point, I turned to Tanaka Sensei beside me and asked him if he knew how many more rounds there would be. He said, 'No more. Now everyone left in final. Congratulations.' I was stunned, but delighted. We were told to prepare for the kumite event, and that the kata final would take place later. When the kumite started, I lined up with the other competitors. Then I heard some people chanting my name from the stands behind me. Surprised, I turned around and saw half of the college students from the *gasshuku* waving at me and cheering. I grinned and waved back at them. It was good to have friends to support me.

Those students gave me a real boost, and I got to the third round of the kumite. In the second round I managed to score an *ippon* (full point) with a mawashi-geri jodan (roundhouse kick to the head). When I did that, Murakami Sensei came running over from the organisers' table to congratulate me. But then, in case I got a cocky, he followed his praise with 'I didn't know you could fight like that.' Back down to earth again...

I was beaten in the third round, despite going a half point up early on. I was using my jab too much, because it had been working well for me, and my opponent just timed me and scored well twice. I was disappointed to be beaten, but I felt I had represented myself reasonably well.

It was great to go out onto the floor with the Honbu Dojo demonstration team. Eric and I were beaten by four votes to three in our jiyu-ippon kumite demonstration competition, but it was all good fun. I also didn't place anywhere in the kata final. In fact, I think I probably came last. But I didn't care; considering the calibre of the other finalists, I was lucky to just be there.

Earlier on Tanaka Sensei had come over and asked me what kata I would do in the final, and offered to help me prepare. I was touched by this sportsmanship, although I am sure that he knew I was no threat to his title. I thanked him for the offer, but I reminded him that he was the defending champion and had to win, whereas I had already achieved more than I expected just by getting to the final. As defending champion, he was under more pressure than the other finalists. He could not afford to lose. I admired his kata greatly, so I genuinely wanted him to win – not that I could have done anything about it. His kata was in a different league to mine. When he did win, I was one of the first to congratulate him.

The previous week during my illness on the *gasshuku*, I had started to question why I was so obsessed with karate, and whether it was worth all the effort. At the championships I was in the stands at one point when I saw Kanazawa Sensei sitting at the top table talking to a dignitary. Three small children approached the table, and shyly asked Kanazawa Sensei if he would sign their t-shirts. Rather than getting annoyed at the interruption and shooing them away, Kanazawa Sensei excused himself from the VIP beside him and chatted warmly for a few minutes with each of the children. Then he meticulously signed each t-shirt, still smiling and talking to them all. He gave every bit as much respect and attention to those children as he had been giving to the VIP beside him. This, I realised, was what it was all about: we train hard to become better people. Like Kanazawa Sensei. I know that no-one is perfect, but I would certainly like to have the patience, kindness and consideration of Kanazawa Sensei, so I still have a long way to go. Karate training requires discipline and patience. It requires many years to make small improvements. It teaches us to be humble. It teaches us to respect others. This is the first principle of karate: to seek perfection of character. While watching his kindness to those children, I knew it was worth every bit of effort, and more.

All the different dojos held parties after the championships. I was invited to the Honbu Dojo party. Most of the referees and officials, as well as the VIPs, were there. Kanazawa Sensei came over to me and congratulated me on getting to the kata final, and thanked me for doing the demonstration. It was another example of how he acknowledges everyone, and treats every person with respect.

After a few more days and only a couple more classes at the Honbu Dojo, it was time to make the long journey home. As I left the Honbu Dojo on the final day, I promised myself that I would be back there again. The experiences in Japan were too valuable to miss for too long.

31. Christoph

Some people seem to light up a room when they enter. It is the same in a dojo. Some people seem to have a greater impact on the spirit in a dojo than others. Their enthusiasm and energy become infectious, and instructors always like to have students like that in their classes.

Christoph von Bültzingslöwen was one such person. He was a German, or more specifically a Bavarian (he loved to tell me there was a difference), who was living in Ireland and studying for a Ph.D. at the local university. When he came to the dojo first, he was already a 2nd Dan from an independent karate organisation and had been training for over ten years. He had been training in a couple of other dojos in Dublin, including a full-contact dojo, and his control was questionable, to say the least, but his talent was immense. He was naturally strong and flexible, and he had perfect technique. He learned quickly, and once shown something was able to do it immediately. He was fanatical about training, and was looking for another place to train to add to the places he already frequented.

He was a gregarious character, confident and loud, with a love of life. The bigger a challenge something was, the more Christoph liked it. When he did his national service in Germany, he joined the parachute regiment because it was the toughest. And he signed up for longer than he had to, just because that was the type of person he was. His confidence sometimes came across as arrogance, and some of the people in the dojo didn't like him when he first joined.

To be fair, a lot of people were on the receiving end of his poor control, so they may have had good reason not to like him. On one occasion, we were lined up with one person facing the line of opponents, each attacking in turn. The person facing the line had to defend and counter-attack. Christoph hit several people both with his attacks and his counter-attacks. I decided enough was enough. I lined up with the others when he was defending. When it came to my turn to attack I hit him with an ushiro-geri (back kick) that caught him straight in the body and lifted him into the air. He landed on his butt, looking up at me, confused. I said nothing, and just went to the back of the line to wait my turn again.

When my turn came around again, I did a different kick – this time it was mawashi-geri (roundhouse kick), and this time it was controlled. The kick just grazed his ear. Again, I said nothing. My third strike was also perfectly controlled. At this point I stopped the class and turned to Christoph. 'Hitting is easy,' I told him. 'I could have hit you all night long like I did with the first strike. The real skill in karate is in *not* hitting. Having control over technique teaches us to have control over ourselves – self-control. This is the dojo *kun*.'

Christoph told me later that although he had been told to improve his control in several other dojos, the message had never really sunk in. We never had any problems with his control, or his attitude, after that. In fact, soon after that, Christoph stopped going to the other dojos and concentrated all of his karate training at Shin-Do-Kan.

When he started training with us at first, Christoph asked me about grading with Kanazawa Sensei. I explained that his current grade would not be recognised by SKIF, because it was not issued by a recognised organisation, so he would probably have to test for 1st Dan again. He dismissed this suggestion, and said that he would instead work towards 3rd Dan in Germany with his old federation. He trained any chance he could, and often asked if we could meet up for extra sessions. He had great energy in every class, and this spread to everyone else. After his slightly shaky start, he became very well liked in the dojo, and it was always noticeable if he was absent.

After training with us for a couple of years and after a few seminars with Kanazawa Sensei, Christoph asked me again about grading with Kanazawa Sensei. I reminded him that, at best, he would have to grade for 1st Dan, or possibly even for brown belt. His reply this time impressed me. He said that he didn't care if he had to grade for white belt. He just wanted to grade with Kanazawa Sensei, because he had so much respect for him. He said that a white belt awarded by Kanazawa Sensei would mean more to him than a black belt awarded by anyone else.

We applied to the national organisation, and because he was so well liked and respected by everyone in SKIF-Ireland, he was given permission to grade for 1st Dan at the next seminar.

The harder the training, the more Christoph thrived. We used to do all sorts of conditioning and stamina training, and I always tried to come up with different things to do in class. We had two heavy punch bags in the dojo, and one night I decided that we should have relay races. I split the class into two groups, and we lined up at the back of the dojo. The first person in each line had to sprint to the top of the dojo and back, passing a baton to the next member of their team, and so on. We used the heavy punch bags as batons! We had to carry it any way we could – over the shoulder was easiest, but some people tried carrying it in their arms. We did several rounds each and, after Christoph passed the 'baton' to the next person at one point, he caught my eye. 'You're crazy!' he laughed at me, obviously loving it. That only encouraged us all to do a few more rounds.

Our syllabus in SKIF is different to what Christoph had been used to in Germany, but he had been training with me for a couple of years by now, so he knew our methods and structure quite well. When he was told he could test for Shodan with Kanazawa Sensei, he worked even harder to make sure that he knew all of the requirements. He trained three evenings a week in our regular classes, at least twice more by himself, and all the black belts usually met at the weekends for extra training. By the time it came to the grading, he was more than ready.

He did an excellent grading. For the previous couple of years he had trained in every single class on the seminars with Kanazawa Sensei. Whether it was white-belt classes or black-belt classes, Christoph didn't care. He just wanted to train. Because of this, Kanazawa Sensei knew him already, and knew his karate was good. When we submitted his paperwork for the examination, I included his grading records from Germany, which showed that he had been a 2nd Dan with that organisation for several years.

Kanazawa Sensei not only passed Christoph for Shodan, but also gave him a rare honour. When he announced the results, he told Christoph that he had passed Shodan, and that he was also going to waive the usual requirement of having to wait two years before testing for 2nd Dan. He said that Christoph could test for 2nd Dan at any time. Christoph didn't understand what Kanazawa Sensei meant, so he came over to me and asked me to explain what had been said. I told him that it was a rare privilege, but that he had been given permission to test for 2nd Dan any time he liked. With his infectious enthusiasm, Christoph exclaimed: 'Maybe next week in London?'

Kanazawa Sensei was standing about ten metres away from us, talking to some people, and obviously overheard him. He turned to us and replied 'Maybe tonight!' and laughed. Then he came over to us and congratulated Christoph on such a good grading. Christoph asked him if he really could grade again soon, and Kanazawa Sensei said he could. However, I interjected at this point and said that maybe he should wait and grade in six months or in a year, when Kanazawa Sensei next came back to Ireland. I explained that Christoph's karate was certainly at 2nd Dan level, but that he would need to study the 2nd Dan syllabus some more.

Kanazawa Sensei turned to Christoph with a twinkle in his eye. 'Your sensei is very strict,' he told Christoph, 'but maybe wise.' And with that he turned and left us to celebrate.

Unfortunately, Christoph never did get to grade again. A few weeks later he had a minor accident on his bicycle. He got knocked off it and banged his head. It was a bit of a bump, but no real harm done, or so we thought. Soon afterwards, he started getting headaches. When these persisted for a few weeks, his father – a doctor in Germany – suggested that he should get a scan to see what the problem was. The scan revealed a large brain tumour. The tumour was not caused by the accident, but had possibly started to grow as a result. He had surgery to remove the tumour almost immediately. It was a very aggressive form of cancer. He received lots of radio and chemotherapy and was quite sick with all of that. He was told not to do any karate because his brain was very tender from the surgery, and he was weak from the treatment.

I visited him in the hospital and at home frequently. We chatted endlessly about karate. He never lost any of his enthusiasm, despite his illness. When Sensei Stan Schmidt came to Ireland, I told him all about Christoph and his love for karate. He insisted on coming with me to visit Christoph, and spent an hour sitting and talking with him. That meant the world to Christoph. He kept looking at me during that visit, shaking his head and grinning at the same time. He couldn't believe that someone like Stan Schmidt would be willing to sit and talk – and pray – with him. I was very glad to have been able to arrange it.

One day, as we were talking, Christoph became pensive for a little while. Then he turned to me and said, 'Do you know why I respect you?' he asked me. I shook my head.

'I have had several different sensei over the years,' he said, 'but I respect you the most. Most of the others that I trained with were good at "training", but you are good at "teaching", and there is a big difference.' I blushed, but he was not finished yet. He continued. 'I know that I am more talented at karate than you are,' he said, without any hint of a boast, 'but you are better than me because you train much harder than I do. That is why I respect you.'

I left his house that day with tears in my eyes. He certainly was more talented than me – by a long way – and I was starting to see how wise he was too.

The tumour was diagnosed in May. The following January, Christoph came to the dojo. The doctors told him that he was in remission. They warned him that this type of cancer usually comes back, so he may as well go and do the things he loves while he could. So he came to karate class.

January is traditionally a month of tough physical training in our dojo, so it was an ideal time for Christoph to be there. It was great to see him back in the dojo again, and for us to feed off his spirit and energy. In one class we were doing slow push-ups, stopping halfway down, at the bottom, halfway up, and at the top. It is a tough exercise, and after only a few repetitions my arms were shaking. I looked around, and everyone was in agony. Yet there was Christoph, looking up at me with the biggest grin you could imagine. He was in agony as well, but he was loving it. I suppose the pain reminded him that he was still alive. I shouted at the class. 'Christoph is grinning at me – these must be too easy. Let's do more!' Everyone groaned and laughed at the same time, but again it was Christoph's spirit that drove us to do more than we thought we could.

The remission didn't last long. At the end of January he was told the tumour was back already, and this time it had spread. The surgeon operated again, but this time he could not remove the entire tumour. More radio therapy and more chemotherapy, but no more training. It was a particularly aggressive tumour, and the doctors informed him that he had only a few months left at the most.

His long-term girlfriend, Olive, told him that she wanted to marry him before he died. The wedding was to be held in Cork, and I was going to travel to it with Kevin Flanagan, one of the senior members in the club. After I set off that morning to collect Kevin and drive to Cork, I got a text message telling me not to make the journey. Christoph had taken a bad turn, and the wedding was being cancelled. The priest that had been due to marry them was instead going to give him his last rites. In shock, I drove to Kevin's house and we sat for a long time in silence, drinking tea. Within a few hours, however, the news was better. The priest came and administered the last rites, but Christoph's condition improved sufficiently for the priest to marry them – with Christoph still in the bed! I am sure that quite a few brave people get married shortly before one partner receives the last rites, but I doubt if many get married *after* one of them has received them! Olive showed herself to be a very strong and brave lady, and cared for him brilliantly throughout his illness. Fortunately, Christoph recovered sufficiently to return to Dublin a few days later. His spirit was not beaten yet.

In April Kanazawa Sensei came to Dublin. Christoph had become stronger again. He was not able to train, but he cycled to the dojo to see Kanazawa Sensei and to watch a class. He was quite weak and thin by now, but his grin was as wide and as infectious as always. He came out for dinner with us that night, thrilled to be sitting and dining with Kanazawa Sensei for the evening.

By way of illustrating the respect that people had for Christoph, the university where he was finishing his Ph.D. allowed his supervising professor to submit the thesis even though it was not yet finished, and also allowed the professor to sit the oral examination on behalf of Christoph. They awarded his Ph.D. just a few weeks before he died. He was very proud of this, and told me, 'At least I will be able to call myself a doctor for a few weeks.'

I visited Christoph as much as possible over the next few weeks. He became more frail every day, and the tumour was now affecting his eyesight and hearing. But his spirit always remained strong. The last time I saw him he was almost unrecognisable. His once-powerful physique was now skeletal. He had lost his eyesight, was nearly deaf, and was slipping in and out of consciousness. Kevin came with me that day. We knew that we were going to say goodbye.

Olive brought us to his bedroom. On the windowsill sat his black belt and just one of the many trophies that he had won over the years. I recognised the trophy immediately. It was the one that he had won with Kevin and me for team kata little more than a year earlier. It was frightening to see how things had changed so much in such a short period. Christoph was in bed, too frail now to move. His once-powerful legs were just skin and bone, and his face looked gaunt.

Olive had to shout to wake him from his slumber. 'Seamus is here,' she yelled in his ear.

'Where? Where?' Christoph said urgently, trying to sit up. I sat beside him. 'I'm right here,' I said, catching his arm. He grinned.

'You look like shit!' I said cheerfully to him. He laughed. 'Same as always then,' he replied. We all laughed, and I marvelled at how he kept his sense of humour throughout his illness. It had often felt like he was looking after us and counselling us, instead of the other way around.

We didn't stay very long. He wasn't able for visitors. As we got up to leave, I told him that I was going, and to take care. This time he did sit up in the bed and faced me.

'*Oss!* Sensei!' he said, with such strength that it was like being back in the dojo. Then he collapsed back down onto his pillow, exhausted from the effort. A karate-*ka* to the end, I thought as I left the house that day, once again with tears in my eyes.

Christoph slipped into a coma the following afternoon and died peacefully a few days later, on the 31 May 2003. He was thirty-three years old.

I had promised him that I would put his picture up in the dojo, so that he would be with us every time we trained. He had loved that idea. His picture is still in my dojo, and those of us who remember him think of him often. He taught me far more than I ever taught him.

Me, Nobuaki Sensei and Christoph. This picture was taken just a few weeks before Christoph passed away.

32. 2004 – London & Scotland

I was kindly invited to attend another seminar in London with Kanazawa Sensei in 2004. Nobuaki Sensei was going to accompany him there, and then continue on to Scotland to teach a seminar for Sensei Jim Palmer. Sensei Ray, Garry and I decided to go to the UK and make the most of the opportunity. This was the first of many trips that the three of us took together.

It is always great to spend time with Kanazawa Sensei, on or off the dojo floor. On this trip we got to do both. We went out for dinner as a group with the seniors from SKKIF – one of the SKIF organisations in England – and made some good friends. Garry is a very entertaining person, and everyone around us fed off his humour so the whole table thoroughly enjoyed themselves.

At one point on the seminar Kanazawa Sensei selected Garry and me to demonstrate some of his kumite syllabus. We did the five-step partner work first, and then we started the three-step (Sanbon) partner work. Kanazawa Sensei has a numbered syllabus, and he explained to the class that there were five different defences for Sanbon kumite. We did Sanbon number 1 first, with me attacking and Garry defending. Then Garry attacked as I did the defences for Sanbon number 2. Then I attacked while Garry did the defences for Sanbon number 3. I was panicking at this stage, because although we knew that there were numbers 4 and 5, at that time I had only ever done number 5 with Kanazawa Sensei and didn't know number 4. Garry knew what my fear was, because he didn't know number 4 either. I started having flashbacks to the seminar a few years earlier, when I struggled with Gojushiho-Sho.

Kanazawa Sensei may have sensed my panic, because as Garry prepared to attack again he said, 'OK, so today not so much time to teach everything, so we will skip number 4, and just demonstrate number 5.' Phew! Garry and I exchanged a quick look of relief, and maybe a little grin, as we went ahead to finish the demonstration. We had a good laugh about that later, but we were worried at the time.

During a break one of the senior black belts came over to introduce himself. His name was Jim Shea from SKIF-USA and he had seen some of my interviews in *Shotokan Karate Magazine* and wanted to meet me. This was the start of another great friendship, and it created the opportunity for me to attend some fantastic training in the USA over the following years.

Later in the seminar Kanazawa Sensei wanted Nobuaki Sensei to demonstrate some of the more advanced partner work, the jiyu-ippon kumite, or semi-freestyle. I was asked to partner with Nobuaki Sensei. I was attacking, and he was demonstrating the various defences.

We had done this a few times before already, so I was reasonably comfortable with it. I always liked partnering with Nobuaki Sensei.

We demonstrated defences 1 to 5 as usual for each attack, which is what we normally did, and what I was used to. Then Kanazawa Sensei announced that we would now demonstrate defence number 6. Again, I panicked. I didn't even know there *was* a number 6! What would I do? Then I remembered that I only had to attack, just as I had done for the first five defences. It was up to Nobuaki Sensei to perform the defence itself. Not knowing what was coming was liberating in a sense. There was no anticipation, and no holding back or protecting myself from the counter-attack in any way. I simply launched my strike with full speed and power.

I didn't even see him move. I felt the kick on my left cheek and only then saw his foot – on the way back down. Before I knew it, he was standing behind me. I was so impressed at the speed, control and movement that I involuntarily uttered the word 'sweet'. All the students in front of me laughed. Fortunately for me, Kanazawa Sensei was behind me, and so now was Nobuaki Sensei, so they didn't hear me and simply thought the students were showing appreciation for the technique. In a way, they were, but part of their appreciation for the technique came from seeing my reaction to being on the receiving end of it.

Demonstrating in London in 2009.

After the weekend seminar in London it was time to travel to Stirling for Nobuaki Sensei's seminar there. Sensei Ray, Garry and I took a flight to Edinburgh, and were collected at the airport by one of the locals. We stayed that night in Edinburgh, and then travelled to Stirling the following day.

We had a great time in Scotland. In fact, the whole trip was simply fun. For example, in Stirling we stayed in a B&B where we shared a room with three single beds. When we went to bed one night, we were still talking and joking so late in the night that we thought the landlady would come in and scold us like naughty children. Fortunately she didn't and we eventually turned out the lights and settled down. Suddenly, Sensei Ray started chuckling to himself again. When we asked him what was so funny now, he replied, 'Ye are too quiet!' and we all started laughing all over again. It was just a silly moment, but it captured the tone of the whole trip.

Nobuaki Sensei was pleased that we made the effort to go to Scotland to train with him. He had taken a train to Blackpool from London. He had taught in Blackpool on the Monday evening, and then travelled to Stirling from there. We told him that if we had known his schedule, we would have travelled with him on the train.

It dawned on me that travelling karate instructors have a difficult life. Their schedule is set by others, both on and off the dojo floor. Where, when and how they travel is usually organised by someone else. The host dojo or organisation sets the training schedule, and sometimes even tells the instructor what they want them to teach. Even where, when and what they eat is often selected by the hosts. I am not saying that it is all bad: of course they are well looked after and are shown a great deal of respect. But a travelling sensei is always working to someone else's schedule, and is certainly not his or her own boss.

I was talking to a famous instructor about this once, who agreed, saying that it could be difficult, what with long flights, jetlag and living for weeks out of a suitcase also being things that people sometimes don't think about. But then he said that the most difficult part was being away from his family so much. He told me that there were times when his children would cry as he left to do an international tour because they knew he would be away for several weeks again, and that he was often in tears when leaving. Being away from home for several weeks at a time – and several times per year – is difficult, no matter how well an instructor is looked after where they go. More and more, I appreciate the sacrifice these professional instructors make to help spread the benefits of karate to those who wish to learn from them.

33. VALDOSTA

In 2004 my company set up an office in the USA, based in a small university town in Georgia, called Valdosta. I really liked it there. The people were friendly and helpful, and it had a good community feel. I tried to visit two or three times a year and looked around for a karate club each time I was in Valdosta, but at first I couldn't find any. Then, a couple of years later, one of the staff said there was a guy teaching karate at the university who was a professor in the Physical Education faculty there. I made contact, and was invited to go and meet him.

Professor Waggener had an unusual first name: Green. And his middle initial was T. The irony was lost on no-one. He told me he liked to be called Tee. Sensei Tee was a 4th Dan in the JKA at the time I met him (he graded to 5th Dan later), under the guidance of Mikami Sensei, based in New Orleans. His wife was Japanese, and she was also a black belt.

I was readily given permission to come and train with them. Sensei Tee kept apologising that their group was mostly made up of university students, many of whom were beginners, but I told him I just wanted somewhere to train, so I didn't care. Actually, there were a few other black belts that used to come along for training too, so we usually had an hour of basic training for the low grades, and then another hour of advanced training for the black belts.

Sensei Tee and I became good friends over the next few years. He often asked me to teach part of the class when I was around, or he would teach a kata and then ask me to show the differences in the SKIF way to do the same kata. He showed me around the university Phys. Ed. labs, and told me about the research they were doing on power generation in the body. He was very interested in the Bo-Jutsu work I was doing with SKIF, and I was often asked to teach. Sensei Tee even gave me a gift of a *jo* (a short staff) that he had hand-carved out of purpleheart wood. It is one of my favourite weapons.

On one of my visits Sensei Tee told me that Mikami Sensei would be visiting Valdosta for a weekend seminar the following year. I decided to make sure that I was in town for Mikami Sensei's visit, as I was keen to meet him. I also asked Sensei Tee if we could get permission for me to interview him for *Shotokan Karate Magazine*. Permission granted, I booked my trip and prepared for a good weekend in the company of another of the original JKA masters.

We collected Mikami Sensei from Jacksonville, Florida, on the Friday evening. He had been travelling most of the day, having taken two flights to get that far. He was hungry, so we took him straight to dinner, which a local karate instructor with us had booked. After

I was introduced to Mikami Sensei he quizzed me intensively about my background and my training with Kanazawa Sensei. I felt like I was the one being interviewed, but I figured he just wanted to be comfortable with me before he opened up.

I was right. By the time we had started the main course at dinner he turned to me and told me I could start the interview. I took out my notes, turned on the recorder, and started what turned out to be the longest interview I had ever done. We talked through dinner that evening, and then through the entire two-hour drive back to Valdosta. Mikami Sensei and I were staying at the same hotel in Valdosta, so we met for breakfast and continued the interview there. During the training he made some interesting points as well, so I took notes after each class to include these in the interview. We talked between classes, and we sat and talked together at every meal.

I apologised to Sensei Tee that I was taking all of Mikami Sensei's attention, but Sensei Tee told me that he was delighted because he was hearing new stories and opinions from Mikami Sensei, and that this was a great opportunity to get him to really open up about many topics.

We talked about his training while Funakoshi Sensei was still alive. We talked about the famous final fight between himself and Kanazawa Sensei at the All-Japan Championships. We talked about some of the pranks and practical jokes they played as trainee instructors, including one time when they put a snake in Nakayama Sensei's bed because he was afraid of snakes! We talked about his relationship with Nakayama Sensei and other great masters. We talked about his move to the USA, and how he survived, then built his organisation there, and the more recent struggles after Hurricane Katrina decimated his adopted home of New Orleans. We talked about some of his controversial opinions on sport karate, other organisations and the openness (or lack of openness) at the JKA. And we talked about a great many other things besides.

I also really enjoyed the training. Mikami Sensei was not a young man, so he didn't do a lot of demonstrating. He gave instructions, and detailed explanations of what he was looking for. It was a very good, technical seminar. But the most memorable part was speaking with him so much, and gaining some real insights into the history of the JKA and his opinions and insights into karate.

The average length of any interview I had done previously was around 3,500 words. When I finally typed up all the notes and recordings and put it all together, this one was over 9,000 words long! It ended up being split into two separate interviews, both of which were published in *Shotokan Karate Magazine*.

34. 2007 – DERRICK'S FUNERAL

It was June 2007 when I happened to go to my office one Sunday evening and found several missed calls from Sensei Stan on my voicemail. Sensei Stan was now living in Australia, and it was unusual for him to call me at the weekend. There was also an email from him. I knew before I read it that something was wrong.

The email was brief and urgent. Sensei Stan had just been told that Sensei Derrick Geyer had died suddenly, and that he was on his way to the airport to fly to South Africa. Sensei Keith, Derrick's brother, was travelling with him. I was stunned. Sensei Derrick was a great karate-*ka*, and as solid as a rock. When I had seen him last he was full of life and mischief. I hated and loved partnering with him at the same time. He was a good friend. I tried to ring Sensei Stan's house, but he had already left for the airport. I then tried to ring Sensei Dave Friend in South Africa but again I got no reply. I had to go home and wait until the next day to find out what happened.

When I spoke to Sensei Dave the next morning he told me that there had been a terrible tragedy and that not only had Sensei Derrick died, but also Sensei Gordon Royffe, who was a little younger than me, and with whom I had sparred on a number of occasions. I felt sick as I listened to the details of the car accident that ended their lives so suddenly. I told Sensei Dave that I was booking a flight immediately, and would be on a plane the following day. He told me that Sensei Gordon's funeral would be on the Wednesday. He offered to collect me at the airport and invited me to stay with him.

The following day I flew from Dublin to London Heathrow, and from there directly to Johannesburg. True to his word, Sensei Dave was there to meet me, but unfortunately my luggage didn't arrive. The airline assured me that it would be there the following day. But the luggage didn't arrive in time for the funeral, so I had to borrow a suit from Sensei Dave's son. When we arrived at the church there was a large crowd from SA-JKA, as would be expected. They were all wearing their blazers and ties, and it was an impressive sight. I was surprised that so many people remembered me: after all, I had not been there for five years, and it was ten years since I made my first trip. Yet they treated me like I trained with them every week, and made me feel like part of their grieving family.

Sensei Stan asked me to sit with him in church. The service was in the traditional Africaans language, but Sensei Stan translated for me throughout. It was a very sombre affair. Sensei Gordon had a wife and young family. It was all very sad.

My luggage arrived in time for Sensei Derrick's funeral, so I was able to wear my own suit. This funeral was even bigger than the one for Sensei Gordon. It was held a couple of days later, and people had travelled from all over the world to be there – from Australia, Europe and the USA – to pay their respects to a man who had helped set the standard for hard training in South Africa. I often had said before that Sensei Keith was the toughest man I had ever faced in the dojo, but Sensei Derrick was the hardest. Where Sensei Keith gave the impression that you could hurt him as much as you liked, but he wouldn't care, Sensei Derrick simply gave the impression that he couldn't be hurt. His arms were like iron bars, and his eyes were like cold steel.

Sensei Keith was naturally devastated at the loss of his brother. They had a very close relationship, even after Sensei Keith had moved to Australia. Everyone wanted to spend time with him to pay their respects, so I just kept in the background to allow him be surrounded by those closest to him. Later in the day Sensei Keith came over to me and we spent some time just talking, like old friends.

Sensei Stan and I went to his house after the funeral. As an outsider, it was interesting for me to see that, even so soon after the funeral, some people were already starting the political manoeuvres to try to get Sensei Stan's blessing to take over from Sensei Derrick's position of chief instructor, which he had held since Sensei Stan moved to Australia. Several people called to the house that afternoon to have a private word with Sensei Stan in order to 'pitch' for the position. I was surprised firstly at how many people felt that they were the best person to take on such a role, and secondly at the insensitivity of the timing of their canvassing. I was also interested to note that none of the most senior people in the organisation were among the 'candidates'. I mentioned my thoughts on this to Sensei Stan. To lighten the mood, we made a joke about it. We decided that Garry Cashman would be the best man for the job, so we rang and asked him if he would like to be chief instructor of SA-JKA. Garry accepted immediately, in the spirit of the mood, and we all had a good laugh.

The Honbu Dojo was closed for the week out of respect. Although we did not train together while I was in South Africa, I spent a lot of time with Sensei Stan. It was good to just talk and be together. I was staying at Sensei Dave's house, and he has his own dojo there. I got up early some mornings and went into the dojo by myself. Each morning I took a couple of minutes just to sit on the dojo floor, contemplating the events of the week and trying to make sense of a senseless, tragic, situation. Then, I would train as hard as I could. It is funny how we can close a dojo and not hold any training, or we can train very hard, and both are perfectly appropriate ways to show respect for the passing of a karate-ka.

I stayed for a few more days after the funeral, attending classes at Sensei Dave's dojo before I left. It felt good, and right, to be getting back to training. Sensei Dave even asked me to teach a class, which the students seemed to enjoy.

A few years later I was having a conversation with Murakami Sensei in the USA, and he told me that he had meant to tell me before that both he and Kanazawa Sensei were glad that I had gone to those funerals, because it was good that SKIF was represented at them. They knew and respected Sensei Derrick also.

35. USA

Speaking of being in the USA with Murakami Sensei, Brendan transferred to his company headquarters in Boston, so he and his family moved there for three years. Although there are SKIF dojos in Boston, none of them were close enough to be convenient for him to attend on a regular basis, so he ended up joining a Shorin-Ryu dojo instead.

That is one of the things I respect about Brendan: whenever he has moved to a different area, he simply has tried to find the best martial arts training in that area and learn from that, rather than insisting on 'Shotokan or nothing'. I am certain that many others, possibly myself included, would have just stopped training when there was no Shotokan available. Brendan trained as a white belt in that dojo for over a year (another quality I like in him: he has little or no ego), before they promoted him to brown belt, and eventually he earned his black belt in their style before he returned to Ireland.

I knew that Kanazawa Sensei regularly visited the area to teach seminars, so I gave Brendan the contact details of Sensei Jim Shea, who has a dojo in Boston. Brendan was invited to go and train on a seminar with Kanazawa Sensei in Rochester, New Hampshire. He got on well there, and they made him very welcome. I decided that I should make the effort to attend the next one. Murakami Sensei was scheduled to teach the next seminar in Rochester, so I arranged a work visit to my office in Valdosta beforehand, and then flew to Boston from there. Brendan collected me and we travelled to the seminar together.

The seminar was jointly hosted by Sensei Jim Shea of Boston, Sensei Mike Cook of Maine and the local instructor, Sensei Steve Warren. They are great guys, and we got on very well from the start. Murakami Sensei kindly agreed to allow me interview him on that trip, so he and I sat and chatted for a couple of hours in his hotel room. Brendan and Sensei Jim were there also, and we were all enthralled with the stories that Murakami Sensei told us. After we finished the interview, Murakami Sensei took out some cheese and drink that he had been given at his previous location and said, 'Now we can relax and just talk. We don't get to see each other so often, so it is nice to catch up.' (It was during this conversation that we talked about my trip to South Africa to attend the funeral.)

I tried to get to the Rochester seminars whenever I could after that. When the Kanazawa No Bo DVD was launched Kanazawa Sensei was asked to include a Bo-Jutsu class as part of the seminars. He agreed, and asked me to teach those classes for him, with him observing and going around the class correcting students. We did this during several seminars.

On one occasion Kanazawa Sensei and Nobuaki Sensei were going to Las Vegas after the seminar in Rochester. My friend Paul Walker, who I had met at the Honbu Dojo on my first trip to Japan and was now living in the USA, had helped organise the Las Vegas seminar, and he invited me to come along for the weekend as their guest.

My wife Nicola and I travelled together with Kanazawa Sensei and Nobuaki Sensei to Las Vegas. We flew first from Boston to Detroit, and then on to Las Vegas. On the first leg of the journey Kanazawa Sensei was flying first class, which he had to do because of his back pain. Before he hurt his back he used to fly economy. Nicola and I had economy tickets, but because of our frequent-flyer status in the USA we received complimentary upgrades to first class. Poor Nobuaki Sensei was left on his own in economy!

Nicola felt sorry for Nobuaki Sensei, so when the cabin crew came round first class with lots of snacks, Nicola grabbed a handful of packs and walked right to the back of the plane to give them to him. And she didn't stop at that. When we got to Detroit, she and I again received complimentary upgrades from the airline. Nicola went up to the ticket desk and told the lady that Kanazawa Sensei was a karate VIP, and that Nobuaki Sensei was a world champion. She asked the lady if she had heard of Bruce Lee, to which the response was 'Bruce Lee? Of course! My husband loves Bruce Lee!' Nicola calmly told her that our travelling companions were better than Bruce Lee, and 'Surely you must have another seat available in first class?' A little charm goes a long way, and within seconds Nicola was handing Nobuaki Sensei a replacement boarding card with a first-class seat beside his father, much to his delight.

Kanazawa Sensei was badly injured in a skiing accident in 2009 and suffers from back, hip and knee pain as a result. People don't realise it because he never made a big deal about it, and continued to travel and teach as much as possible. But on that flight to Las Vegas I saw him doubled over with pain, and Nobuaki Sensei looked very worried about his father.

Nicola came to the rescue again. She had a couple of strong painkillers and a heat patch that we gave to Kanazawa Sensei, and it offered him enough relief to be able to get some sleep on the flight. Of course, when we got to Las Vegas he never complained about being in pain, and patiently sat signing autographs or stood for photos for anyone that wanted one, and taught every class with the energy and vigour of a man in the prime of his health. He truly is a great man.

The USA, and particularly Rochester, had become a second home, and I made a lot of friends during seminars there, with people from all over SKIF-USA and Canada. I loved that the senior instructors there were all as interested in the Bo-Jutsu and T'ai Chi teachings of Kanazawa Sensei as they were his karate teachings. I was very honoured to be involved in helping them with that, and delighted to take part in many T'ai Chi classes with Kanazawa Sensei, and to do my fourth and fifth T'ai Chi grading examinations with him there.

Sensei's Jim, Mike and Steve even organised to bring me to Rochester to teach a couple of seminars. It worked well because I could combine it with a business trip to my office, which kept the costs down. I visited New Hampshire and also Montreal several times in this way. Unfortunately my work in the USA dried up and the office closed, which in turn curtailed my travelling to the seminars in the USA – at least for a while.

Demonstrating in USA in 2009.

36. 2008 – JAPAN

In 2008 we proved that dreams can come true. It started with a phone call. It was May, and I had just received an email telling me that the SKIF thirtieth anniversary would be celebrated in Japan that October. There was to be a seminar, a function and grading examinations. So I rang Garry. I had been to Japan several times already, but Garry had never been, and it was his dream to make it there one day.

'Here's one for you.' I didn't even say hello when Garry answered the phone. He listened in stunned silence as I proposed that we take a little trip later in the year.

'Not a chance!' was his initial reaction. 'Impossible! It will cost too much, and I won't be able to take that amount of time off work.' He didn't believe that he (or we) could make it happen. But Garry knew that I didn't believe in impossible. Not only was I determined that we get to go, but also that we would get to do a grading examination together in Japan.

Over the next couple of months we both worked to overcome the various obstacles, and by August we had succeeded in clearing the way. We had even persuaded Sensei Ray to come with us. I made the travel arrangements. I was very excited about this trip, partly because it would be Garry's first trip to Japan, but also because I would get to share the trip with two karate-*ka* I thoroughly respected. The three of us were on the same wavelength: we loved karate training, and that would be our focus. We would go to all the classes we could, and we would make the most of this opportunity to experience Japanese culture first-hand.

Garry and I were granted permission from the organisation attempt the Godan (5th Dan) grading examination in Japan. This was a big deal for both of us. I had already done my Yondan (4th Dan) examination in Japan several years earlier, but it is always special to test in Japan. Garry was especially pleased. Just a few months earlier he thought that a trip to Japan was an impossible dream, but now it was actually going to happen.

The night before we left Sensei Ray and Garry came and stayed at my house because we had an early flight, and my house was close to the airport. There wasn't a lot of sleeping done, because we stayed up late making plans for what we were going to do during the trip, and then we had to get up at five to go to the airport. But who needed sleep? Armed with tea bags and chocolate, we were off to Japan for serious training and a lot of laughs.

Even though Sensei Ray had been to Japan several times in the past, this trip was different. For his previous trips, there had always been a specific agenda, such as a World Championships. This was his first time going there just for training and to experience the country, and his first time without the responsibility of looking after a group.

I was able to organise funding for the accommodation, so we checked in early at the luxurious Keio Plaza Hotel in Shinjuku and got a couple of hours rest before heading out to experience a bit of Tokyo; then it was off to the SKIF Honbu Dojo for our first training session.

Training at the Honbu Dojo is always special, but the first time is always extra special. Garry was like a child at Christmas when we got to the dojo. We were early. In fact, Murakami Sensei had just arrived and opened up the dojo, so we were able to look around and enjoy the peace before anyone else arrived. Every dojo has a special atmosphere, whether it is a humble school hall or a full-time dojo, but it is an exceptional experience to visit the Honbu Dojo of whatever association you belong to. It is the karate equivalent of making a pilgrimage. We certainly had a sense of that on that evening. Although I had done this several times already, we knew that we were privileged to be able to make such a trip together.

Murakami Sensei gave a great class. There were many other visitors there, as well as quite a few locals. People from the international SKIF community had started to gather in Tokyo for the anniversary celebrations, so it was natural that there was a large crowd at the dojo. Three of the senior foreigners were selected by Murakami Sensei to teach a short section of the class on a topic of their own choosing. It is an honour to be invited to teach at the Honbu Dojo. The chief instructor from Belgium, the chief instructor from Chile and Sensei Ray were selected, and each taught a different aspect of training for about ten minutes. It was most enjoyable.

After the class Murakami Sensei invited about twelve of us to go out for a meal with him, so we spent the next few hours in good company. Garry kept looking at me as if to say, 'I can't believe that we are really here'. We had permanent grins on our faces.

There were about 250 black belts from Japan and around the world at the weekend seminar. It was great, as always, to see so many members of our karate family. All of the Honbu Dojo instructors were there, assisting Kanazawa Sensei because of the large numbers of students, and also teaching or demonstrating different segments themselves.

On the last day we were doing some Jiyu-Ippon Kumite (semi-freestyle). One of the defences involves a jumping kick. Kanazawa Sensei was saying that people were not getting up high enough and not doing the kick properly. He was close to me and seemed to stop to watch, so I felt under pressure to execute the technique well. I launched myself into the air and extended my kick a fully as possible. Unfortunately I extended too much, and felt an excruciating pain in the back of my leg. I knew immediately that I had torn my hamstring. Kanazawa Sensei had turned away before I hit the ground, but I collapsed in severe pain. Murakami Sensei saw me drop to the floor, and immediately sent someone to go and get ice.

I had to sit out the rest of the training session, but that was the least of my worries. I was due to test for 5th Dan the following day, and I knew that this was a serious muscle tear. Sensei Ray, Garry and I were all very subdued as I hobbled back to the hotel. I followed the proper procedures for treating a torn muscle, but the following morning the whole back of my leg was black and blue from the internal bleeding, which confirmed the extent of the tear. Walking was painful. I didn't know if I would be able to do any karate.

I was reluctant to tell Sensei Ray and Garry that I didn't think I could do the examination, because Garry was due to test with me that morning. I knew if I withdrew from the examination that he would not want to do it without me. We had trained together for so long and had come this far together. So I said nothing, and went to the dojo with them: had I been alone I may not have gone.

There was a large crowd at the dojo as a lot of students were grading that day. The atmosphere was tense but exhilarating. Garry had given me a bandage and I strapped up my leg tightly. It felt a little better, or maybe adrenalin was starting to mask the pain. Or maybe I was just fooling myself. I went and spoke to Nobuaki Sensei, and asked him if he thought I would be able to make adjustments to the techniques in my kata. He looked surprised, and asked why: I showed him my leg and he winced. He suggested that maybe I could ask Kanazawa Sensei to make a special allowance for me. I thanked him for the suggestion, but something made me decide not to ask for special favours. This was the Honbu Dojo, with some of the most senior grades in the organisation present. If I wanted 5th Dan, I was going to earn it properly. I was in a lot of pain, but I knew that the pain was temporary. I also knew I would regret it later if I asked for special treatment. As always, I wanted to *earn* my grade or not get it at all. I recalled feeling that I had not properly earned my 3rd Dan.

I made my decision, and all the nerves and fear vanished immediately. I would not ask for a special allowance. I would not make adjustments to the kata. I would do the full examination and deal with the pain later. I walked over to Garry and said, 'Let's get this done.' It was the most positive and determined I had felt since the previous afternoon.

Garry grinned at me. 'We've come too far to stop now,' he told me, and he was right.

It seemed that the next couple of hours were spent warming up and cooling down again. There were a lot of people grading for the lower Dan grades, so it was a long time before we were called out onto the floor. When we eventually went out to do our basics, I managed to ignore any pain and focused only on getting the karate right.

I had a fright during the first part of the examination, which was a combination of basic techniques. Kanazawa Sensei stopped us after a couple of repetitions and asked me to do one part of the combination again. I thought I must have been doing it wrong, and was desperately trying to figure out why, but it turned out that he wanted me to demonstrate it for the person beside me because he was the one not doing it correctly. Phew...

After the basics, we had another long wait before being called out again for kata. This involved another cycle of warming up and cooling down, which was not doing my leg any good. However, when we were called out again I completely forgot about my injury and just did the best kata that I could. Then we demonstrated the *bunkai* for the kata. Adrenalin is a powerful thing. I didn't feel any pain while on the floor going through the grading itself. The lower grades all had kumite to do: Garry and I were also all set for kumite, but it was not required, and neither was the special demonstration we had prepared.

After the examination was over we all lined up for the results. Quite a few students in the lower grades were told to try again. Others were told that they would get the result later, as further deliberation was necessary. Only about 50 per cent of students were being told that they had been successful.

My name was called out, followed by 'Pass'. Relief. Then Garry's name was called out. Kanazawa Sensei said 'Pass', but then retracted that and said 'Oh sorry, result later.' We were stunned; we thought that he had done a good grading.

It was lunchtime by the time we had showered, changed and left the dojo in a very sombre mood. Garry was naturally disappointed, and Sensei Ray and I sympathised. It was strange that when we walked into the dojo that morning they were feeling bad for me, and on the way out we were feeling even worse for Garry. We were low for the whole afternoon. Garry didn't really want to talk to anyone, but at the same time he felt guilty about not celebrating my success. But then again, none of us felt like celebrating. We dissected the whole examination over and over again.

We had to cheer up by evening as we were attending the formal function to celebrate the thirtieth anniversary of the organisation. On went our best clothes and best smiles, and off we headed to the function room. Shortly after our arrival, we got talking to Suzuki Sensei, one of the Honbu Dojo instructors, who congratulated me on passing my grading. I took the opportunity to ask if he knew what Garry had done wrong. He looked surprised and said that he thought Garry had passed. He went to check the paperwork, and came back a couple of minutes later to say that yes, Garry had passed: it had been a mistake. Now we could celebrate! Our mood immediately turned to delight. In fact, we left the function room and went to the main hotel bar for about an hour, where we drank several jugs of hot saké.

Over the past fourteen years, since we started training together at my new dojo, Garry and I had become 'brothers in karate'. We had been through a lot together. As we chatted in that hotel bar in Tokyo, we reminisced about how far we had come and how much we had somehow managed to achieve over the years.

The following day, our last in Japan, we went to the dojo in the morning for a final training session. My leg was very sore, but I didn't want to miss my last day at the Honbu Dojo. Tanaka Sensei taught the class. We expected that perhaps he would give us a tough time, being our first class after the grading, but he didn't. Instead, he gave a wonderfully technical kata class, in which we were reminded just how much we still have to learn. After the class Tanaka Sensei and Nobuaki Sensei took us out to lunch as their treat, and then we had to go back to our hotel and pack for the long journey home.

37. 2008 – Making the DVD

Once the contract for the Kanazawa No Bo DVD was finalised I set about organising how to get it made, and engaged the services of a professional movie production company. They told me that I would have to do a storyboard and a script before we even started (things about which I knew nothing) and we looked for suitable locations to do the filming. Eventually it was decided that the best thing to do was to build a fake dojo in a movie studio and do the filming there. I wanted cameras at multiple angles so that we could easily show the kata from different sides. There was an enormous amount of work and planning to be done before we even got near the cameras.

Kanazawa Sensei and Nobuaki Sensei came to Dublin for the filming, just one week after Sensei Ray, Garry and I had been in Japan with them. I collected them at Dublin Airport and brought them to my home. I had a little surprise in store, because I had had a dojo built at my house, which had been completed a few days before they arrived. I was hoping that Kanazawa Sensei would teach the first class in my new dojo. I also had my 'crew' lined up: Sensei Ray, Garry, and my students, Kevin Flanagan, Alan Cleary and Dara Clear, all of whom were going to help on the DVD.

When we arrived at my house I welcomed Kanazawa Sensei and Nobuaki Sensei and showed them around, leaving the dojo for the end of the 'tour'. When they eventually saw it, they were very surprised and impressed, and Kanazawa Sensei readily agreed to teach a class there that evening for me.

There were ten of us in the class: all those who were going to help with the DVD, plus another of my black-belt students, and my five-year-old son, Conall! It was Conall's first time putting on a karate suit, and he was – for once – very shy and refused to do very much, but I didn't care. I was delighted that his first-ever karate class was with Kanazawa Sensei, and that it took place at our home dojo. In fact, Kanazawa Sensei announced at the beginning of the class that the first class at a dojo was always a special occasion. He said that he would teach part of the class, Nobuaki Sensei would teach part of the class, and that I was to also teach part of the class. It was an incredible memory for us all. After Kanazawa Sensei finished teaching his segment and Nobuaki Sensei took over, Kanazawa Sensei lined up with the rest of us and simply trained alongside us! The spirit and inspiration he exuded was like nothing I had ever experienced before, and we all kept looking at each other in disbelief. For my part, it was a dream come true – and then some.

Kanazawa Sensei trained beside us while Nobuaki Sensei led part of the first class at my new dojo, 2008.

Drinking Sakē together after the first class in the new dojo.

Nobuaki Sensei working with the Bo while Kanazawa Sensei observes the class.

Kanazawa Sensei demonstrating his Nunchaku skills.

When it came to my turn to teach, it made sense that I would use it as a rehearsal for the filming work the next day, so we worked on the Bo kata and *bunkai*. Again, Kanazawa Sensei and Nobuaki Sensei joined in and trained with us. I was glad of the opportunity, because I wanted to show Kanazawa Sensei some of the ideas I had for the filming and to ask him a few questions. We got everything sorted, and it was a training session that will never be forgotten by those who were there. To top it off, we drank saké in the dojo after class to mark the occasion before all going out for dinner together.

The next day we travelled to the film studio in Dublin, where problems became immediately apparent: they had built the set too small, which meant that we were not going to be able to fit everyone in the way we wanted, and we could not use cameras at the sides as I had planned. It was very frustrating, but we had to make adjustments to the plan and keep going, because this was our only allocated day for filming.

We ran quickly through what was going to be covered, making the necessary adjustments and checking the camera angles. Then we started the filming itself, with the first part being for us all to line up with Kanazawa Sensei while he introduced the DVD. After his part in front of the camera finished, he got to sit and supervise the rest of the filming. There were many times over the next seven hours where he said the words that are familiar to all karate students: 'One more!' And so we would do it again, and again, and again. When he was satisfied, we moved on to the next section.

My hamstring was sore from the injury just one week earlier in Japan, but I managed to get through the morning's filming with minimum pain. Unfortunately I cooled down over lunch and the hamstring tightened up; and straight after lunch I had to perform Kanazawa No Bo Sho. On the first take I felt a stab of pain, and I knew I had made the injury worse. There was nothing to be done though, and I had to keep going. Whether it was because of the pain, or maybe I was nervous in front of Kanazawa Sensei (and the cameras), but I kept messing up the kata, and had to do it about eight times before I got one that he considered good enough. It even got to the point of having to ice the hamstring in between takes!

Eventually, having completed all the filming , we could relax. The Japanese instructors were staying at my house again that night, so we went out for dinner and they expressed satisfaction with the day's work.

In my naivety, I thought that we had the bulk of the work done for the DVD, but I was very wrong! When it came to the editing we realised that of the four cameras that we had used on the day, only one of them produced footage of good enough quality to actually use. That meant that we now didn't have everything we needed to make the DVD. Fortunately, none of the footage involving the

Japanese instructors was affected, but it meant that, two months after the initial filming, we had to go back to the film studio, rebuild the 'dojo' set, and film various sections all over again. And after that, we had all the editing to do. The film production company had great facilities for this, but we still spent over a hundred hours editing all the footage, putting it together, recording and inserting voiceovers, adding effects and music.

When the DVD was finally finished we held a 'premiere' as part of the launch. We invited all current and former students from the dojo, as well as people from other clubs and arts, a couple of local politicians and people from the press to a drinks reception, followed by a showing of the DVD. On the night of the premiere a man at the reception bowed and said 'Oss Sensei!' as I walked past. I didn't recognise him, but returned the bow and kept going. A few minutes later I asked one of my students if he knew who the man was. He didn't, so I forgot about it. A little later, the same man approached me again and bowed once more. This time I stopped to talk to him.

'You don't recognise me,' he smiled.

I admitted that I didn't. He looked like he was in his mid twenties, and had a full beard. I figured that maybe the beard was making it difficult to identify him. Then he told me his name and I instantly remembered him. But the person I remembered was a boy of about twelve, who had trained with us for maybe six months many years ago – and here he was now, a grown man.

He told me that it was thirteen years since he had been a member of the karate club. He was now twenty-five, had graduated college and was working. The invitation to the event had gone to his parents' home, but he happened to see it and wanted to come along to say hello. He said that, over the years, he often thought of the karate training and the lessons I taught. In particular, he told me that he remembered me saying 'If it were easy, anyone could do it,' and, 'Most worthwhile things are difficult to achieve – that's what makes them worthwhile.' This principle of working hard had helped him get through college when he found it tough. Even though he had only trained for a relatively short time when he was quite young, the lessons and benefits of karate training had helped him greatly many years later.

That short conversation, and the fact that he had gone to the trouble to come and thank me, made me realise that we often don't know how much we are helping people through teaching them karate. Even when people stop training, they may still benefit from our lessons. For me, that was the highlight of the evening.

I was so sick of all the work we had done filming, re-filming and editing the DVD that I couldn't even watch it. When the lights dimmed and the DVD started playing that evening, I closed my eyes for the entire thing! In fact, it was only about four years later, when my son asked me if I would watch it with him that I actually sat through it.

Fortunately it was well received, and people really didn't notice all the little things that I was still not happy about. It got good reviews in various magazines and blogs, and – more importantly – people bought it!

The trouble was that I had spent far too much on the project, and it was going to be difficult to ever break even, let alone make a profit. I didn't mind so much. After all, not many people get to make a DVD with Kanazawa Sensei, and I would have preferred to lose money and do a good job, than to make money on an inferior job.

38. IF YOU BUILD IT

The time when Kanazawa Sensei came to stay at my house was very special. Several years earlier I had bought some land to build a house. My business was doing very well at the time, so it seemed like a good investment, although times became a little tougher later. I hired an architect: he studied the land, looking at the elevations and aspect. Then he asked me about what I liked to do and what I wanted in a house.

I told him that karate was my passion, and that I really wanted my own dojo. Once I had explained what a dojo was, that became his starting point for designing the house. Then I also told him that it was a dream of mine to someday have Kanazawa Sensei come and stay at my house. Again, I tried to explain just how much of a VIP Kanazawa Sensei is in the karate world, and how important he is to all his students.

I had been to other people's houses with Kanazawa Sensei. He sometimes commented that it was nicer to stay at a house with a family (as long as he knew them well) than to always stay in hotels. Anyone who travels a lot for work will know how boring and lonely hotels become after a short while, and very few people travel as much as Kanazawa Sensei did for many years.

The architect listened to all of this, and determined that I was looking for a guest suite for Kanazawa Sensei or other guests, which should have the comforts of a hotel, but should also be homely and enable guests to feel part of the family. Perfect! Except then I said that Nobuaki Sensei often travelled with his father, so perhaps we needed a second one as well...

'No problem,' replied the architect. 'We will put one at each side of the house.'

And so the house was designed around a beautiful dojo in the basement and two guest suites on the top floor. General living and family bedrooms were sandwiched in between on the ground floor. The larger suite was named the 'Kanazawa Suite' and the slightly smaller one was named the 'Nobuaki Suite' long before either of those gentlemen ever set foot in them.

If you have ever seen the movie *Field of Dreams*, then that is what it was like when we built that house. 'If you build it, he will come,' is one of the key quotes in the movie, and that is exactly what happened. In planning the DVD production I also ensured that the dojo was completed just days before Kanazawa Sensei and Nobuaki Sensei arrived to stay. They each stayed in the rooms that bore their name; they were able to relax and have fun playing with my young children, but they had their privacy as well. They taught in my dojo, and we even mounted a plaque on the wall to commemorate the occasion. It all worked out exactly as I had hoped.

Tick another one off the bucket list.

Kanazawa Sensei with my son, Conall,
at my house in 2008.

39. ATHENS

The SKIF World Championships took place in Athens, Greece, in 2009. I was not participating in the championships, but Kanazawa Sensei had asked me to go there to promote and sell the new Kanazawa No Bo DVD. Nicola and I flew to Athens like travelling salesmen, armed with a suitcase full of DVDs, polo shirts and posters.

Before the championships there was a training seminar with Kanazawa Sensei, assisted by several of the Honbu Dojo instructors. I try not to miss a chance of training with Kanazawa Sensei, so naturally I went along for the training.

Kanazawa Sensei started off getting the instructors to demonstrate his kumite syllabus, starting with the kihon (basic) kumite, and then moving on to the jiyu-ippon kumite (semi-freestyle). Murakami Sensei and Nobuaki Sensei demonstrated the jiyu-ippon kumite. Then we all worked with partners on various aspects of these exercises. Towards the end of the session, Kanazawa Sensei said he wanted the jiyu-ippon kumite demonstrated one more time. Everyone sat down again in a large circle as he signalled to Nobuaki Sensei to come forward. I was sitting down, waiting for Murakami Sensei to go forward also, but Kanazawa Sensei pointed to me and asked me to join Nobuaki Sensei in the centre. I was slightly surprised, but having often partnered with Nobuaki Sensei, I was comfortable enough to be on the receiving end of his impeccable techniques.

It all went very well – as always. I sat down again afterwards, still slightly confused to have been asked out to partner with Nobuaki Sensei, but always delighted of the experience of working with him. We can learn by watching such demonstrations, but when we get to experience the techniques at first hand, it is learning at a different level.

Later in the seminar we split into groups to work on various kata, with a different Honbu Dojo instructor for each group. I was in a group doing Sochin, but I was also keeping an eye on the people next to us where Murakami Sensei was teaching Nijushiho. He was making a very interesting point that slow moves can contain speed, sometimes starting quick and slowing through the move. He was demonstrating this beautifully in a way that I still struggle to replicate.

At the end of this session Kanazawa Sensei had us all sit down again, and this time invited students to go out and demonstrate the various kata that had been worked on. They were to do this in a group, so everyone doing a particular kata would all go out together.

As this seminar was the precursor to the world championships, a lot of people who were hopeful of doing well in the kata competition were keen to go out and get in some extra practice and maybe some constructive criticism. I remained seated, as I was not participating in the championships, and felt it would not be fair to go out with those who were competing.

One thing that surprised me was that when the group went out to do Unsu I was disappointed with what I saw. Several of those who demonstrated the kata did what I could only describe as a technically poor kata, albeit with a spectacularly good jump. It was as though they had neglected the entire kata in order to work on perfecting the jump. To me, this was missing the point: it is a kata with many unique techniques, and with wonderful rhythm and timing. Some of the best demonstrations of Unsu I have ever seen have not had a particularly athletic jump, but the entire kata has been done with real intent and focus. I often think about those people doing Unsu when I work on my kata, and try to ensure that I don't fall into the same trap.

Later that evening I was back at my hotel and about to go out for dinner. As I walked past the bar I saw that Kanazawa Sensei and the Honbu Dojo instructors were inside having a drink. I stopped for a minute to say hello and pay my respects.

Kanazawa Sensei turned to me and thanked me for partnering with Nobuaki Sensei earlier in the day. He told me that Nobuaki Sensei liked to partner with me. I figured this was because we were similar height and build, which makes partnering easier, and because we knew each other well at this stage, having partnered together a lot at various seminars in different countries. I told Kanazawa Sensei that he didn't have to thank me, because it was always my pleasure to partner Nobuaki Sensei.

Over the next few days we were very busy selling the DVDs and merchandise at the championships. At various points, Nobuaki Sensei, Daizo Sensei and other Honbu Dojo instructors came and sat at the stand with us, signing autographs on the items that people bought. I was surprised at this, but Nobuaki Sensei told me that I was helping SKIF, so they had to help me too. I am always impressed at how considerate all the instructors are, and how quick they are to express their gratitude.

40. SKIF BO-JUTSU

Some time after the launch of the Kanazawa No Bo DVD, I visited Scotland again to train with Kanazawa Sensei, as I often did. We got talking about Kanazawa No Bo, and how we could encourage more people in SKIF around the world to become interested in studying it. It became apparent that we were discussing more than just a pair of kata; we were talking about a full system that complements the karate system of SKIF. Once we had reached this conclusion, Kanazawa Sensei suggested that we should develop a proper syllabus and have a grading structure for Bo-Jutsu within SKIF. He asked my opinion of this, and I told him that it sounded very exciting. Then he asked me how many grades there should be. I thought about it for a minute, and then suggested that we should do it like T'ai Chi, which Kanazawa Sensei had already been teaching in parallel with karate for many years. In T'ai Chi there are six levels, so I felt it would be good if Bo-Jutsu had the same. Kanazawa Sensei agreed with this suggestion, and we then discussed the basic structure of a syllabus. I was asked to expand on this work, and to then come to Japan a couple months later, in October 2010, to formalise the syllabus with Kanazawa Sensei.

With the SKIF Honbu Dojo instructors in 2010.

I spent a week in Japan on that trip, training as much as I could at the Honbu Dojo in the regular classes. But I also took part in the instructor training, where the syllabus and grading structure were finalised with Kanazawa Sensei and taught to all the Honbu Dojo instructors. It was a great privilege for me to be there and be part of that.

The grading structure is based on the Tai-Chi structure of six levels. It is intended that students should already be at least Shodan in SKIF karate before testing in Bo-Jutsu, so the first level, or grade, in SKIF Bo-Jutsu is approximately equivalent to Shodan in karate. This grade is called 'Sho-Kyu', meaning beginner level. The second level is called 'Chu-Kyu', meaning middle level, and the third is called 'Jo-Kyu', meaning high level. These are the three 'student' grades. After this is 'Shidoin', which means instructor, and is a formal instructor qualification. The fifth level is called 'Jun-Shihan', which approximately means 'below master'. The final level is 'Shihan', the master level.

For our work in developing the Bo-Jutsu system, Nobuaki Sensei, Murakami Sensei and I were all automatically awarded the grade of 'Jun-Shihan'. The other Honbu Dojo instructors were awarded the rank of 'Shidoin'. It was necessary to do this in order to establish the authorised instructors and examiners to be able to go and teach Bo-Jutsu for SKIF. Only Kanazawa Sensei held the highest grade. I actually felt aggrieved to be awarded my grade without having done a grading examination, but as this was the birth of the new system I understood that it had to be done this way.

The following month the first formal international SKIF Bo-Jutsu seminar and grading examinations took place in England, as part of a regular SKIF karate seminar. Kanazawa Sensei and Nobuaki Sensei taught the karate classes, and I taught the Bo-Jutsu classes, with Kanazawa Sensei and Nobuaki Sensei carefully overseeing my teaching. Some of my students travelled from Ireland to take part in the first ever SKIF Bo-Jutsu examinations. People from Scotland, England and Spain also participated in those first examinations.

Kanazawa Sensei conducted the examinations, with Nobuaki Sensei and me sitting with him. He made sure to ask our opinions on the students' performances before he made his decisions. We all knew that he didn't need our opinion, but he is always a gentleman and wanted us to be involved, and to learn how he conducts such examinations.

For me it was yet another chapter of what seemed like a surreal experience. I knew that we were witnessing an historic occasion in the life of Kanazawa Sensei and SKIF. He was already a legend in karate, and an acknowledged master of T'ai Chi. Now he was establishing his own system of Bo-Jutsu, and we were there to witness it and be a part of it.

I feel very lucky and privileged to have had the opportunity to help with this work on SKIF Bo-Jutsu in a small way, to support Kanazawa Sensei and the other SKIF Honbu Dojo instructors. I am also very fortunate to be able to travel to different countries to teach Bo-Jutsu, which I do several times a year.

41. Spirit of the Empty Hand

Over the years I recommended the book *Spirit of the Empty Hand* to a lot of people. However, the book was now out of print, and became more and more difficult to purchase. Second-hand copies of the book were advertised online for anything up to US$250! I sourced a few copies from time to time from a second-hand online bookstore in South Africa. One day I received an email from the bookstore telling me that they had something that might interest me. *Spirit of the Empty Hand* was originally written as the thesis for Sensei Stan's Masters Degree in Communications. Only eight copies of the thesis were ever printed. One of these had now been purchased by this bookstore, and they were selling it. I immediately agreed to buy it.

It was signed by Sensei Stan and dedicated to his former assistant, thanking her for her help in editing the thesis. When he came to Ireland I showed it to him; he was stunned, and readily wrote in it for me.

People who knew of my friendship with Sensei Stan sometimes contacted me to ask where they could get the book, and I often sent people one of my spare copies. When I ran out of spares, I contacted Sensei Stan to ask if he had more. Unfortunately, he had also run out. I asked him if he could contact the publisher to see about getting the book reprinted. He did so, but the publisher did not consider it viable.

Rather than give up, I then suggested that perhaps we could get it reprinted ourselves, if the publisher would allow it. The original book was great, but it had a significant number of typographical errors and the binding sometimes caused the pages to come loose. I felt we could improve it if we could republish it. Sensei Stan spoke again to the publisher, who gave permission for us to republish the book. I was thrilled! I knew that there was still a demand, and that a lot of people had never had a chance to read it simply because it was not available.

We decided to bring it out as a limited-edition hardback, with each copy individually numbered and signed by Sensei Stan. We re-edited the whole book, correcting all the typographical errors. Then I contacted my old friend Maurice Richard Libby from Canada, and asked him to produce some illustrations to go with the new edition. We worked with a publishing house to organise the hardback binding, dust jacket and a box sleeve for the whole package.

During the final stages of production, Sensei Stan surprised me with a request. He had written a new epilogue to go with the book, and he asked me if I would write a new foreword. I was stunned, but delighted to contribute to a book that meant so much to me.

The book was published as a special collector's item. It was expensive to produce, so it was not a cheap product, but it was still cheaper than most of the second-hand paperback versions available on the internet.

It was surreal to me that I was able to become directly involved with a book that had been at least partly instrumental in keeping me from quitting training when my friends were dropping out, and which enabled me to become friends with one of the great karate masters of the world. At least it was available once more, and seeing it listed on the website of the world's largest online bookseller gave me an immense feeling of satisfaction.

42. PINK KARATE

A few years ago I had an idea to raise money for charity. After Christoph had passed away from a brain tumour, I had wanted to do something to assist cancer charities. It occurred to me one day that the 'pink ribbon' symbol for Breast Cancer Awareness looked a little bit like a pink karate belt. Of course, there is no such rank as pink belt in karate, so I wondered if we could get some pink belts made and if people would buy them and wear them for a good cause. It was September, and October is Breast Cancer Awareness month, so the timing seemed good. I used social media to investigate the idea, asking people what they thought. The response was overwhelmingly positive, so I started looking for a supplier of the belts.

I found a company based in the USA that said they could supply pink belts. I placed an order for fifty belts, and started promoting 'Pink Karate – Breast Cancer Awareness'. The idea was that I would pay for the belts myself, but when selling them the proceeds would go to charity. Within days I had orders or queries for more than the fifty belts that I had ordered, so I placed a second order with the company, this time for two hundred belts.

The first fifty belts arrived, and I distributed them to those who had ordered first. The company was promising me that the rest of the belts would arrive soon, but days turned to weeks, and assurances from the supplier turned to silence and unreturned phone calls. It soon became apparent that there was a problem. When I eventually managed to speak to someone, they told me three different stories about why there was a delay. I had lost all faith in them at this stage, and anyway October was now almost over so I contacted my credit card company and got them to cancel the transaction and refund my money.

I brought some of the few belts I had left from the first batch to Japan, and I had pictures taken with all of the SKIF Honbu Dojo instructors wearing them. When they saw the belts at first I could see them thinking 'I'm not wearing that!', but as soon as I explained the reason for it they all put them on with no hesitation and were happy to pose for pictures.

Unfortunately, quite a few people were disappointed that year, having either ordered belts or told me that they would order them. Of course, anyone who ordered belts but didn't receive them got a full refund, but I still felt I had let people down, despite my efforts.

I was going to drop the whole idea completely, but was in Canada a few weeks later at a seminar with Kanazawa Sensei and Murakami Sensei. We were taken to a martial arts goods supplier in Montreal who told me that they could easily make the pink belts for me within a few weeks. I decided to give it another try. This time I ordered one thousand belts in six different sizes. It was November, so we had eleven months to get organised before the following October. Again, promises from sales people didn't turn into delivery. I had been told I would have the belts by April. In the end, I had to tell the company in September that if I didn't have the belts by the beginning of October I would require a full refund. Even then, I didn't actually receive the belts until nearly halfway through October. But eventually they did arrive and I was able to get them out to people.

After that, things started to go more smoothly. The idea was that people would buy the belt, and the proceeds would go to a Breast Cancer charity. Then, simply by wearing the belt they would raise awareness, because the belts were very noticeable as something unusual and made people ask what they were about. Awareness helps lead to early detection, because it reminds people to do regular health checks, and early detection saves lives. But I also encouraged people to do a sponsored 'Pink Karate' event in their club, and raise money for their local cancer charity. Then I encouraged them to take pictures and send them in to their local papers to raise awareness again, with the added bonus of generating free publicity for their club.

Soon people were posting pictures all over social media with their pink belts. One club in the USA sent me an email with pictures, saying they had raised nearly $1,000 in sponsorship for a local cancer charity simply by wearing their pink belts in class.

I had pictures of quite a few students and senior instructors wearing the pink belts, so I thought we could do a calendar with pictures of people wearing the belts. We did one in 2012 with Kanazawa Sensei, Sensei Stan Schmidt, various SKIF Honbu Dojo instructors and groups all with their pictures in it. Again, I put up the money for the calendar, with the proceeds to go to charity. Unfortunately, the calendar sales were poor, and I would have been better off just donating the cost of the calendars to charity in the first place. I thought I might try it a second year, with the idea that I would get more groups to submit pictures, and if we got a lot of group pictures then everyone who was in each picture would want at least one copy of the calendar. I sent a note with each belt sold, asking for pictures to be sent in. But I got very few pictures back, so I had to give up on that idea.

Still, more and more people were buying and wearing the belts, and posting pictures online and spreading the word. Over the coming years I even saw that other groups were getting their own pink belts made and wearing them in October as well, making their own donations to charity.

However, despite some difficulties along the way, it has been worth overcoming the obstacles. It has been far more successful than I thought it would be when it started. With the money that I received from selling the belts, and the money that people raised and sent directly to their local breast cancer charities, tens of thousands of euro have been raised and donated to various cancer charities through the idea of Pink Karate.

43. SIMPLE PLEASURES

Kanazawa Sensei is great company when he is able to relax with people he knows. I have been fortunate enough to stay in the same hotels and houses with him on many occasions. I have seen him relax and enjoy himself, and he enjoys a good laugh as much as anyone.

On one occasion, Kanazawa Sensei and I were staying at the home of Sensei Jim Shea in Boston. While Sensei Jim and his wife were cooking a barbeque dinner for us all, I sat and watched Kanazawa Sensei casually doing T'ai Chi in the garden. He wasn't doing it for show, or to teach, or even as serious practice; he was simply killing time and stretching his legs before dinner. But it was superb. I remember thinking that if I could just once in my life do T'ai Chi as well as that, I would be happy.

After a lovely dinner on the patio, the evening was getting cooler, so we moved to where the brand new fire pit had been lit. Sensei Jim was delighted with his new toy, and was keen for us to try it out, and I had bought some giant marshmallows to toast on bamboo skewers. The trouble was, I had never toasted marshmallows before (it is not an Irish thing – toasting marshmallows in the rain has little appeal), so the first one I attempted caught fire and had to be thrown into the flames. The second one melted too much and got a bit too gooey, so it slid off the skewer into the pit as well.

Kanazawa Sensei was laughing at my attempts, so I said he should have a go, and handed him a skewer and marshmallow. Actually, we all just laughed and had fun, and I believe more marshmallows went into the fire pit than got eaten that evening. Sensei Jim pretended to protest that he was going to have to scrub the pit clean the next day because of all the burned marshmallows sticking to the bottom, but then his marshmallow fell into the pit as well!

We eventually did get the hang of it and managed to eat some toasted marshmallows. Kanazawa Sensei, who had never had them before, declared that they were delicious. Sometimes it is the simplest of things, and good company, that provide the best of memories.

44. TEACHING SEMINARS

Over the next few years more and more SKIF students all over the world actively participated in Bo-Jutsu seminars and examinations, and the movement continued to grow steadily. I had the privilege of teaching Bo-Jutsu classes on seminars with Kanazawa Sensei in several different countries. On one occasion, after teaching a seminar in the USA in 2010 we were walking back to our hotel rooms together and Kanazawa Sensei said, 'I enjoyed watching you teaching today.' Naturally, I was pleased that he seemed to approve of my teaching, but I admitted to him that it made me very nervous to teach anything while he was watching. 'Yes, I know,' he replied with a chuckle and a grin, as he disappeared into his room.

I began to travel to different countries to teach Bo-Jutsu seminars by myself. By now my business was struggling due to global economic difficulties, so I made the decision that, instead of subsidising my karate club as I had for eighteen years, the karate club would have to subsidise me. I therefore became a semi-professional instructor, taking a small wage from the dojo for the first time. I still had to work though, so I tried to limit myself to teaching weekend seminars only, to minimise the disruption to my normal working week, even if this often meant taking the Friday and Monday off work in order to travel to and from the seminar.

But I was not complaining. It is always very enjoyable to teach something new, and I tried to make the seminars interesting and fun, while hopefully also showing people how training in Bo-Jutsu could help improve their karate. This was the original reason that Kanazawa Sensei studied Bo-Jutsu, as well as other Kobudo (weapon arts), and T'ai Chi. With the Bo, he studied traditional Bo-Jutsu, and developed his own kata and system so that karate students could easily relate to and learn from it. This, therefore, is always the main theme of my seminars.

As soon as we had conducted the first grading examinations in Bo-Jutsu we were approached by several countries keen on hosting seminars. Sensei Jim Palmer in Scotland had attended and graded at the first seminar, and he immediately asked me to travel to Scotland to conduct a seminar for his students. I have been there every year since then. I also travelled to Montreal with Kanazawa Sensei and Murakami Sensei shortly after we conducted the first examinations in England, and we held the second group of examinations there, this time for students from Canada, USA and Mexico. The instructors from Montreal and USA had been enthusiastic about having Bo-Jutsu classes as part of their seminars for the previous few years, so I was very glad that they were among the first to get to take the grading examinations. Over the next few years, I travelled several times to both Rochester in New Hampshire and to Montreal.

A couple of years later, Richard and Michel – the instructors in Montreal – asked permission for me to join Murakami Sensei on his annual seminar with them, to teach Bo-Jutsu and Tai-Chi. Murakami Sensei very kindly agreed to this. The event was so successful that Murakami Sensei suggested to Richard and Michel that this should become an annual event, with both of us going there together. This was a very generous suggestion from Murakami Sensei, to allow me to join him and do some teaching, and I was very grateful, as always, for the support that I was receiving from the Honbu Dojo instructors. We have done that seminar together for several years now, and it seems much appreciated by the students.

Other countries were now also seeking to hold Bo-Jutsu seminars, so I was making about eight teaching trips each year, plus taking another one or two trips abroad to train with the other instructors. International travel is not always straightforward though. Having had my suitcase go missing in the past, I always make sure to bring a karate-*gi* and my belt in my hand luggage when I travel.

On one occasion, I was travelling to Ukraine to teach my annual weekend seminar there. Despite the fact that I was travelling from one European country to another, I had to take three flights to get to my destination, L'viv. This meant taking Friday off work and being at Dublin airport at about 5:30am. Because of fog in Frankfurt – my first stop – we were delayed leaving Dublin. I was worried about missing my connecting flight from Frankfurt, but the airline kept telling me that it would be ok, because flights out of Frankfurt were also delayed. They didn't seem to understand when I told them that I had a further connection. Sure enough, when I finally got to Frankfurt, my connecting flight to Vienna was delayed and it looked like I was going to miss the flight from there to L'Viv. I tried to get the airline to change me to a different route, but they just kept telling me that there were lots of people on the flight who had the same connection in Vienna, so they would hold the flight for us.

Needless to say, they didn't hold the flight. It had taken off before we even landed in Vienna. The people at the customer service desk told me that the next flight to L'Viv was the next day, so I would have to stay in Vienna for twenty-four hours! My only other option was to take a flight to Kiev, and make my own way from there. I contacted my hosts in Ukraine, and they advised me to take the flight to Kiev, as some of the people participating on the seminar would be driving through Kiev and could collect me.

I arrived in Kiev after 11pm that night, several hundreds of kilometres from L'Viv. I was collected at the airport by guys who were driving a beat-up transit van. They asked me if I wanted to ride in the front or in the back. I was surprised to be offered the back, but then they showed me the sofa they had tucked in there! I chose to stay in the front, with a proper seat and a seatbelt.

Although Kiev is a mere 550 km (340 miles) from L'Viv, it took a long time to get there. Roads were not in great condition, as Ukraine is not a wealthy country. Driving in the van with people sitting on a sofa in the back was slow enough. Also, they had driven several hours from eastern Ukraine to get as far as Kiev, so they were already tired. After a few more hours of driving, we pulled in at a cheap hotel to rest – from about 3am until 6:30am – and then we were off again.

It was lunchtime on Saturday by the time we finally arrived in L'Viv. We were supposed to have had a two-hour class in the morning and then another two-hour class in the afternoon. I suggested to my hosts that we do four hours in the afternoon to make up for the lost time, and they were delighted with that. I was tired, naturally, but glad that we were able to make up the lost time for the students on the seminar. It had been a difficult journey, but it was interesting to get driven halfway across Ukraine, and I had been very well looked after once I got as far as Kiev, so I couldn't complain.

At one point, my day job took me to South America and I spent a bit of time in Argentina, Brazil, Paraguay and Uruguay. It was great to be able to go and train with the local dojos in the various countries, but in Argentina they organised for me to do some formal seminars as well. I visited two years in a row, and by the end of my time visiting there I was able to conduct Bo-Jutsu grading examinations for them.

In spite of the occasional flight hiccups, I know it is a privilege to travel to different countries and teach seminars, and I always enjoy meeting up with old friends and making new ones.

45. European Championships 2014

The SKIF European Championships were held in Dresden, Germany, in 2014. I had not been involved with the Irish team since I retired from competing in 2001. However, about a month before the team were due to travel to Dresden I was approached by the chairman of SKIF-Ireland and asked if I would take on the role of team manager for the event. This is an administrative role, not to be confused with that of coach. My role was to take charge of the day-to-day tasks, such as helping to sort out the buses, hotel rooms, training space and times, and dealing with issues as they arose at the event. It is a role intended to free up the coaches and competitors to focus on the competition itself. I agreed to give it a try, although I was concerned that I had been away from the competition scene for so long that I might not be much help. But the job was straightforward enough, and was more about organising skills than competition, so it suited me.

As I was going to the event anyway, it was then suggested that maybe I could take part in the competition itself. I felt that I didn't have the preparation behind me to take part in the kumite event, but that it might be nice to compete in the kata event. My attitude to the competition surprised me. I wasn't concerned at all; in fact, I didn't even decide which kata I was going to choose until the morning of the event itself.

There were nearly fifty competitors in my category. I think they call it the Masters category these days, but it used to be called the Veterans. They split us into two pools of twenty-five. Each competitor could choose their kata. The top four from each pool would go through to a semi-final, and then four of the eight would go through to the final. Despite little preparation for the tournament, I was pleased to make it comfortably enough into the top four in my pool and so reached the semi-final, but I didn't make it to the final. At least I had maintained my personal goal of never being beaten in the first round of an event, and I was satisfied that my standard was still reasonable. More than anything, I enjoyed meeting up with the competitors and officials from all around Europe. I had forgotten how useful events like this are for networking and socialising.

At one point, Sensei Antonio Racca from Switzerland and I were walking together in the stadium, and passed a stand where some of the Swiss team were having a beer. Sensei Racca asked me if I would join him for a round. As I don't generally drink, I politely declined, saying that maybe we would have a drink another time. Sensei Racca smiled at me and said, 'OK, no problem. But I am your *Sempai* – if I ask you a second time you cannot refuse.' I agreed, while secretly making a mental note to try to avoid him near the bar in future!

I started to walk away, but had covered no more than a few steps when I heard Sensei Racca call my name. I stopped and turned to see him grinning at me. 'Seamus, will you have a beer with me? I am asking you a second time!'

I could only laugh and shrug my shoulders, knowing I was beaten. I walked back as all the Swiss team cheered and Sensei Racca grinned, and I drank a beer for only the second time in my life. (The first time had been many years earlier when Kanazawa Sensei bought me a beer when we went out for a meal after training in Japan. I didn't want either of us to lose face by refusing it, so I drank it.) In both cases it wasn't that I felt pressurised into drinking, and I don't have any moral objection to it. It was more that both times the drinks were bought out of genuine kindness and camaraderie.

46. C.W. Nicol

Sensei Stan asked me a few years ago if I had details for C.W. Nicol, as he had lost contact with his old friend. I didn't, but I said I would try to get an email address for him. I found his official website and asked for C.W. Nicol's email address, but after two weeks I had still not received a reply. Then I sent another email, saying that I was looking for the address on behalf of Stan Schmidt, and within two hours I had a message back from C.W. Nicol himself, from his personal email address. I was delighted to receive an email from the author of *Moving Zen* – my all-time favourite martial arts book. Although I was tempted to write back, I resisted and I passed his details on to Sensei Stan and left it at that.

Some time later I received another email from C.W. Nicol, thanking me for putting him back in touch with Sensei Stan. He told me that Sensei Stan had talked to him about me, and that he would like to meet. The next time I travelled to Japan we tried to arrange to meet up, but he is a very busy person and his schedule didn't allow it. We tried to make arrangements each time I travelled to Japan, but something always seemed to prevent it: actually, we *had* agreed to meet up on one trip, but he was called away at the last minute to advise the government in Ethiopia on conservation. I reluctantly conceded that this was somewhat more important than meeting me...

I am not one to give up easily, so when I arranged yet another trip to Japan I contacted him and told him the dates I would be there. I was in luck: he was available for a couple of the days that I would be there, and he invited me to come and visit. Sensei Ray was with me on that trip, so C.W. Nicol – who prefers to be called Nic – invited us to visit his home and nature reserve in the mountains near Nagano.

On a beautiful spring morning in Tokyo we sat under the *sakura* (cherry blossoms) in real danger of getting sunburnt. At lunchtime we took the *Shinkansen* (bullet train) from Tokyo to Nagano, and then a local train to Kurohime. The weather changed dramatically as we travelled, and by the time we got to Kurohime we were glad that we had taken Nic's advice and packed warm clothes. It was cold and wet, with more than a metre of snow on the ground.

Although the weather had become colder and wetter, it did nothing to dampen our spirits. Sensei Ray and I had chatted excitedly for a good portion of the journey in between rereading snippets of *Moving Zen*. We were very much looking forward to finally meeting the man who inspired so many with his writings.

We took a taxi from the train station to the local *pension* hotel, a beautiful little place called Tatsunoko Pension, run by a friend of Nic's. He had booked rooms for us there. As soon as we entered the building, we spotted Nic in the lounge. He came to greet us and welcomed us to his remote part of Japan, cheerfully pointing out that life here was very different from in Tokyo. We agreed, telling him that it had been hot and sunny in Tokyo that morning! We talked for hours, eating a wonderful dinner at the hotel, part of which Nic cooked himself. In Japan, he is famous for his documentaries, cookery programmes and more than a hundred books on many different topics.

Nic readily agreed to be interviewed, but really all I did was set up the voice recorder and record the hours of conversations we had together. He entertained us with stories of his adventures around the world. He impressed us with his passion for conservation. He treated us to some songs and poetry that he had written. The karate world knows him as the author of *Moving Zen*, but he has done so much more than that with his life. He has recorded music albums and sung in concerts with famous opera singers. He has had run-ins with the *yakuza* (Japanese mafia). He has met with heads of state and been awarded various honours, including an MBE from the Queen of England. And yet, the thing he cares most about is his beloved nature reserve – the C.W. Nicol Woodland Trust – in the heart of the mountains. He took us there the following day, and we witnessed his work first hand. Of course, we were most interested in talking about karate, which is still very much an integral part of his life.

When we left Kurohime and travelled back to Tokyo on the *Shinkansen*, Sensei Ray and I were pinching ourselves. We couldn't believe how welcome Nic had made us. It had been a dream for both of us for many years to talk with him, and when we finally got to meet him he treated us like lifelong friends.

47. Preparing for 6th Dan

I was becoming better known for teaching Bo-Jutsu than karate, and for me this was a bit of a problem. One karate instructor even asked me if I only did Bo-Jutsu or if I also did any karate! Karate has always been my main art, and despite my emphasis on Bo-Jutsu and T'ai Chi when I teach seminars, I always train much more in karate than I do with the Bo.

I believe that when we pass a grading, then we have to train at a new level. We have to put ourselves under pressure not only to deserve the grade we have, but to strive towards another level as well. I dislike the notion of just going to the dojo and training in the same way year after year, and then seeking to grade again when the required minimum time has expired.

After I passed my 5th Dan examination I automatically started working on different concepts and playing around with various kata with the vague intent of preparing for another grading sometime in the future. It was not that I was in a hurry to grade again, as I already felt that I held a higher grade than I deserved or ever thought I would have. It was more about setting challenges and always trying to improve myself. Perhaps this is a sign of a competitive nature, but the competition was within myself rather than with others.

I was working on a few kata in the dojo by myself one day, and almost without realising it, found that I had selected two on which to focus for my next grading, although it was at least a couple of years before I would even be eligible to test. So I worked regularly on these kata in my personal training. During class, I also spent more time teaching these kata to my black-belt students, because I always find that teaching something helps me to analyse and understand it better. Interestingly, over time the one that I thought would be my first kata became my second kata, and vice versa. I couldn't say when this happened exactly – it just evolved that way.

Meanwhile, Brendan had been training with the University of Limerick Karate Club for a couple of years, and they asked him if he would take over as the club instructor. Having been training for nearly thirty years, he had somehow managed to avoid becoming an instructor until then, but he liked the university club and it worked well for him, so he agreed to do it.

One of the things that the university students do every two years is to organise a trip to Japan for the karate club students and instructors. After Brendan took over as instructor he brought me in to teach seminars and provide advice to the club, so I became a member too. In January 2014 I was able to travel with the group to Japan for twelve days. I try not to miss any opportunity to train with the Japanese instructors, and training in Japan is always a good way to put myself under pressure.

Being students, the accommodation was a youth hostel. Brendan and I shared a tiny room with bunk beds – something we hadn't done since we were very young! We were about an hour from the dojo, but that was not a problem. Getting around Tokyo is never a problem as the train system is very efficient.

I had been to Japan many times already, but always either by myself or with one or two others only. This time there was a larger group of around twelve people, and we all stuck together. There was a great atmosphere. Despite the fact that Brendan had been training in karate longer than me, this was his first time in Japan, so it was good that we were able to do that together. Apparently some of the university students had only intended to visit the dojo a few times during the trip, but when I told everyone about my training plans – every day, and sometimes twice a day – they all trained more than they had originally planned.

My next trip was just a few months later, in April 2014. This time I was part of a delegation from SKIF-Ireland to attend the first SKIF International Seminar in Tokyo. This was a very impressive three-day event, with over 450 people attending from all over the world. The seminar was split into three groups for most classes, with 1st Dan and 2nd Dan in one group, 3rd Dan and 4th Dan in a second group and 5th Dan and above in the final group. The instructors rotated between the groups, giving everyone the opportunity to train with each of the instructors. Kanazawa Sensei taught several advanced classes during the seminar, which was impressive for a man who was nearly eighty-three years old and had constant back pain.

For one class, they split the groups differently and announced that Murakami Sensei would take one group and that anyone could take part, but that we should only do so if we were willing to do a very tough class, and that people with health problems should avoid the class. Anyone not willing, or able, to join in could go into one of the other groups. Sensei Ray and I took one look at each other, shrugged, and immediately went straight over to where Murakami Sensei was waiting with a grin on his face. I was surprised at how few joined us. Maybe Sensei Ray and I are just gluttons for punishment.

Before we started, Murakami Sensei repeated the warning that this would be very difficult. He said it would only be one hour, but that people should feel free to go to another group if they wished. It was a class of basics. Simple enough, but very high intensity: fast, high-energy and lots of repetitions. Within five minutes I was wondering if I had made the right decision. I was having flashbacks to the *gasshuku* I had done in Japan more than a decade earlier, and also the Early Birds training in South Africa. But I knew if I could get through those, I could get through an hour of this.

Murakami Sensei laughed. 'I will make you happy! This class will make you happy!' he roared, as he did every exercise along with us. We doubted it very much, already too tired to argue. We started another exercise – switching from left-front stance to right-front stance in one spot while doing gyaku-zuki (reverse punch) – and did fifty repetitions. Then we did fifty more. It was all done at the pace of a sprint, and while facing a partner so neither person could slacken off.

'I hate this exercise!' shouted Murakami Sensei, grinning as he said it. 'Fifty more!' And so we did fifty more. Of course, he was making a point. The exercises we don't like are often the ones that are most beneficial, so they are the ones we should do most of all. The class continued at that pace throughout. Everyone was sweating hard. Most were puffing and panting. There were red faces all around me, and I knew mine was probably the reddest of all. People felt like they were going to vomit. From time to time, someone would stop and move to the side to recover, before joining back in again, but no-one quit. Eventually, we were told we were on the last exercise, and everyone dug deep to finish strongly. Then Murakami Sensei took us through some light stretching. Everyone felt relieved and exhausted, but also elated. We were grinning from ear to ear.

'I told you I would make you happy,' grinned Murakami Sensei. 'You are happy that the class is over!'

We stayed ten days in Japan on that trip, training every day, and spending time in the evenings with the various groups from the different countries. We loved the idea of the annual international seminars, and everyone looked forward to attending them in the future.

I was personally hoping to make it to the international seminars each year, although I knew that was probably unrealistic. Then it was suggested by one of the instructors that perhaps I should go to the second seminar, in April 2015, and grade for 6th Dan. That settled it for me: I was definitely going. I figured that three trips to Japan in fifteen months, plus all the seminars I attended elsewhere, plus the seminars that I taught myself in various countries and all the training I did at my own dojo, all probably added up to reasonable preparation for a grading. But still, I increased the intensity of my training significantly over the coming months in preparation for the next trip to Japan.

My flight to Japan was a disaster. Bad weather in Amsterdam was causing chaos. I missed my connection, as did thousands of other passengers. I queued for hours at customer service just to have them re-book me onto another flight. Eventually they put me on a flight to Shanghai, and from there to Tokyo. I landed in Tokyo twelve hours later than my original scheduled arrival time. Never mind, I thought. I might still make training at the Honbu Dojo, if I went directly there. I knew class started at 7pm. I didn't think I would make the beginning, but if I could get there before the end I would still bow in and get some of the training. I was hoping class finished at 9pm.

I took the Narita Express into Tokyo, and then changed trains, taking the Yamanote Line to Gotanda. There I had to change again to get a train to Kugahara, dragging my luggage with me. It all took longer than I had expected, and it was almost 8.30pm by the time I got to Kugahara. The dojo is very close to the train station, so I hopped off the train and ran: even if I could get the last ten or fifteen minutes of class, it would be better than nothing.

I arrived at the dojo just in time to see the final bow through the window. I was gutted. The other Irish guys were there (they had taken a different flight) as were a lot of people from various countries. I went in to apologise for my tardiness, and to greet the instructors and all my friends: they all gave me a hard time, saying that I would go to any extreme just to avoid training. The joking was just what I needed to get over such a stressful journey.

Over the next few days I made up for missing that class at the Honbu Dojo. The seminar followed a similar format to the previous year, although there were fewer people. That was logical – people could not afford to come every year, but most people were hoping to make one out of two, or two out of three. I was trying to maintain a quiet focus about the grading, which would take place at the end of the seminar. I knew several of the people who were also testing that weekend, so there were a few nervous faces at the seminar, as people dealt with the stress of the upcoming examination in their own way.

The night before the grading there was a party for everyone at the seminar. One of the instructors wished me luck for the examination the next day. As he said it, it occurred to me that I was not so worried about the examination for myself, but that I wanted to do a good job for Kanazawa Sensei. He has dedicated his life to teaching karate to us all, with infinite patience. What I wanted most was to go out on the floor and do a good job for him to see that I had learned something – anything – from him. I wanted to do this grading for him rather than for me.

In my work, I have given presentations to large groups of people. I have negotiated large contracts with multinational corporations. I have sat in board meetings with CEOs. None of that ever fazes me. But Kanazawa Sensei makes me nervous: because I respect him so much, because he has done so much for me and for many others, because he has set such a high standard for himself and for all who follow his way, it is always daunting to stand in front of him. Having to teach a class with him watching, or having to do a grading examination in front of him, no matter how many times I have done so, always makes me feel like a novice in front of the master. It seems like he can see right through me; that he can anticipate my mistakes before I even make them. He knows all my strengths and weaknesses before I even walk onto the floor.

And that is how it felt when I did the grading. Although there were several of us on the floor at once, I felt like his eyes were boring through only me. All I could do was focus on my breathing to keep everything under control, and I got through it as best I could.

There was an anxious wait after the examination finished. I knew I had done as well as I could have, but I just was not sure if it was enough. As the results were being announced, several of the students were informed that they would have to try again another time. I started to feel that I might be joining them. Then my name was called.

'Seamus O'Dowd.'

'*Oss*! Sensei!' I stepped forward. Kanazawa Sensei looked up at me with a stern look that seemed to last forever. My heart sank. Then he smiled.

'Roku-Dan,' he announced with a grin, knowing that he had terrified me with his look. I bowed and heard people clapping. I had passed.

That evening, a large group of us went out for dinner and a few drinks. I was relieved to be finished with the grading, and could now enjoy the rest of the trip.

The following day we were enjoying the annual *Hanami* (flower-viewing picnic), sitting once again under the *sakura*. Nobuaki Sensei spoke to me and asked me what I thought of some of the extra elements they had included in the examination, where they tested the Dan grades on parts of the Kyu-grade examination syllabus. I replied that I thought they were good, and that I felt it was important that everyone should continuously practise the entire syllabus. He told me that their intention was to make the Dan grading examinations a little more difficult, especially for the higher Dan grades. I told him that he could make them as difficult as he liked now, because I was already a higher grade than I ever thought possible, so I was finished now and would never grade again! He laughed.

It felt good to go training at the Honbu Dojo over the next few days with no examination to worry about. Training in Japan is always enjoyable and intense, but it is easier to enjoy it after an examination than before.

*

On the flight home from Japan I realised that I was only a few months from my thirtieth karate anniversary. I reflected on the time I was a white belt, watching my brother perform Tekki-Shodan and thinking that I could never learn that. I remembered the phone call telling me that I passed my Shodan examination. I remembered the feeling of nervousness when I opened my dojo. I remembered many highs and lows over the previous thirty years.

Karate went very quickly from something that I *do* to something that I *am*. It is a constant struggle, because there is no shortcut or easy way for serious karate. It is a path: a *Do*. But it is worth every second, every drop of sweat, and every injury. Karate has helped me in so many unexpected ways, so much more than the mere physical ability of defending myself. People often ask me if I have ever used my karate, and I tell them that I use it all the time: in the calm determination that is required in business negotiations and boardroom meetings; in studying the body language of a difficult customer; and in everyday life by being aware of what is going on around me so that I can avoid ever having to actually engage in a dangerous situation.

I often wonder what my life would be like without karate. There are people I went to school with who were great athletes then, but who are now overweight, unfit and inactive. They talk about the glory days of the past, while I still feel fit and strong, and look forward to continuing to improve.

Karate has helped make me the person that I am – hopefully a person of integrity and character. I have many flaws, but they are more under control because of karate than they would be otherwise. I will always be a work in progress, and this is why my karate journey will never end.

As my brother said to me at the beginning, it doesn't get easier. But it is worth it. I estimate that I am probably about halfway through my karate 'life'. I have now been training for thirty years, and still have a long way to go. I am looking forward to the next thirty.

AFTERWORD

I thought I knew young Seamus – now Sensei Seamus – pretty well. I have spent many enjoyable times both inside and outside of the dojo training, and also sharing ideas and witticisms with him and his lifelong friend Garry Cashman. And I have had the pleasure of meeting his sensei, Ray Payne.

I also know that *A Karate Story* would not have come into existence without the inspiration and charismatic leadership of Grandmaster Kanazawa, founder of SKIF, whose amazing way of life is well depicted in this book. I was privileged to train under Sensei Kanazawa when I first visited the Japan Karate Association in 1963 and was impressed then, as I am today, by his amazing skills, innovative ability and warm demeanour.

But reading Seamus's book made me realise that I had been looking at the mere tip of the O'Dowd iceberg. As the story unfolded I found it fascinating to see how a youngster who was well below average at sports, and far removed from the excellent achievements of his two older brothers, suddenly changed gears at the age of sixteen and, with his nose to the grindstone of karate, moulded himself into the accomplished karate exponent that he is today.

Not only is he accomplished, but Seamus is also a very likeable guy with a sense of humour that is second to none. I still smile at the time he sent me a white belt as a birthday gift: in addition to that, he and Garry Cashman also wrote and sent me a booklet with a title to parody my book, by calling it *Spirit of the Empty **Head***, in which they poked fun at themselves, at me, and at different aspects of karate. I have had people in tears of laughter as I read them sections of this little gem. It included lists of alternative book titles, such as *Mooing Zen – Philosophy for Cows* and *The Pessimist's Guide to Karate: Spirit of the Half-Empty Hand*. Between them, they have a unique way of combining irreverence with a genuine sense of respect for all karate-*ka*, and a love of their chosen art.

Every beginner, student and high graded karate-*ka* should read *A Karate Story*. Not only does Seamus address the techniques and fighting spirit of karate, he more importantly reveals to the reader the ethos that underlies the serious practice of karate: camaraderie, kindness, humility, respect for our fellow karate practitioners and for all human beings, all of this juxtaposed with those constant and necessary cousins: courage, challenge, extreme pressure and innovation.

As I enjoyed reading his words and fascinating experiences it gradually dawned on me that Seamus was most certainly not an overnight karate wonder. The beauty of this warm-hearted karate story is that it starts with a youngster who was basically a dropout at school sports. He was a stay-at-homer who, despite his brother's success in karate training was not interested until he reluctantly took a karate class at the age of sixteen. Something happened in that one class to make him want to do karate of his own volition, and from then onwards it was just blood and guts that gradually transformed Seamus, that reluctant and shy boy, into a dynamic and respected karate champion and instructor. This did not happen over months, or even years. It took decades of honestly applying the maxim: Train man, train!

I have seldom come across a more dedicated practitioner of the art who is prepared to reach out and study other martial arts such as T'ai Chi and Bo-jutsu to enhance his prowess in his chosen art of karate.

Stan Schmidt
Melbourne
October 2015